A
CREATIVE GUIDE TO
Cross Stitch
Embroidery

A
CREATIVE GUIDE TO
Cross Stitch
Embroidery

NEW
HOLLAND

New Holland (Publishers) Ltd
24 Nutford Place, London W1H 6DQ

ISBN 1 85368 122 9 (hbk)
ISBN 1 85368 251 9 (pbk)

Editor: JO FINNIS
Designer: PETER BRIDGEWATER
Cover designer: PETER BRIDGEWATER; PAUL WOOD
Photographer: STEVE TANNER
Illustrators: JOHN HUTCHINSON; GEOFF DENNEY;
ANDY WATERMAN; JO FINNIS
Phototypeset by CENTRAL SOUTHERN TYPESETTERS, EASTBOURNE
Originated by SCANTRANS PTE LTD
Printed and bound in Hong Kong by SOUTH CHINA PRINTING CO LTD

AUTHOR'S ACKNOWLEDGEMENTS
. . . .

The author would like to thank the following:
DMC for supplying embroidery fabrics and threads and
needlework accessories
Cara Ackerman of DMC Creative World
Wendy Bailey
Nigel Benson of 20th Century Glass
Charlotte Parry-Crooke
Clare Royals
Gillie Spargo

CONTENTS

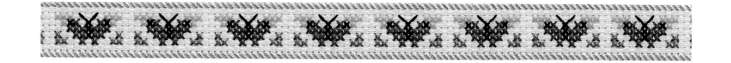

CHAPTER ONE

HISTORY & DEVELOPMENT

INTRODUCTION

The first stitches were used to join animal skins to make clothing. The first textiles were probably crudely constructed from grass and other plant materials, until a way was found to twist fibres and animal hairs into continuous strands by spinning. From about 10,000 BC until the development of synthetic fibres in the twentieth century, the raw materials for textiles came from four natural fibres: wool and silk from the animal world and cotton and flax from plants.

Embroidery probably began as a means of strengthening a fabric by darning in extra threads, then developed gradually into the decorative process we know today. Fragments of cloth dating from between 5000 BC and 500 AD have been excavated in South and Central America, Egypt and China, and these show crude examples of darning, half cross stitch and satin stitch. Many of the fragments are linen; the regular weave of this fabric, one of the oldest of woven materials, provided the basis for the development of counted thread stitches. Over many centuries embroidery has been practised by both rich and poor, amateur and professional, and used to personalize household linen and possessions; to enrich domestic and ecclesiastical garments and accessories; to decorate furnishings and add ornament to ceremonial robes and banners.

THE ORIGINS OF CROSS STITCH

The earliest example of cross stitch is thought to

date from about 500 AD. The design is worked completely in upright crosses on linen, and the fragment was discovered in a Coptic cemetery in Upper Egypt. Very few pieces of decorated fabric have survived from ancient and early Christian civilisation, but this does not necessarily mean that decorative stitching was rarely used. Natural fabrics are perishable and do not survive as well as the many metal and ceramic artefacts found in archaeological sites.

There is not yet sufficient evidence available to enable us to trace the exact origins of cross stitch embroidery. Some historians suggest that the development of cross stitch owes much to the craftsmanship of the Chinese, since cross stitch embroidery is known to have flourished during the T'ang Dynasty between 618 AD and 906 AD. It is quite feasible that these cross stitch designs and techniques subsequently spread from China via India and Egypt to the civilisations of Greece and Rome, and from there throughout the countries of the eastern Mediterranean and the Middle East. An alternative school of thought suggests that the spread of cross stitch embroidery may have been in entirely the opposite direction, since the first important migration of foreign people into China took place during the T'ang Dynasty. Persians, Arabs and travellers from Greece and India followed the silk routes to China and many eventually settled there. There is some evidence to suggest that these immigrants influenced the designs used in Chinese arts and crafts, particularly those for textiles. Many Chinese textiles bear motifs that show great similarity to those found on Persian fabrics.

EARLY SAMPLERS were used by needlewomen to experiment with stitches, techniques and designs. They later became exercises in education, giving children practice in spelling and stitching skills.

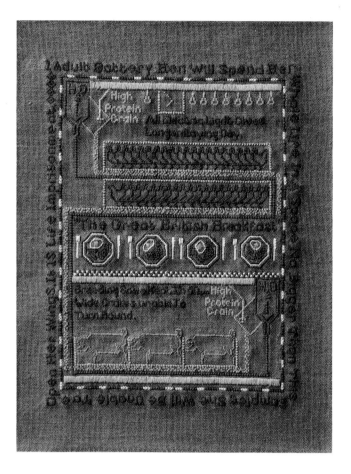

*MODERN STITCHERS often adapt
traditional sampler techniques to get a
message across in a novel way. This sampler,
stitched by Susan Beckett, graphically
expresses the horrors of factory farming.*

What is certain, however, is that the techniques and
designs of cross stitch spread from many of these countries throughout the European continent. The Crusaders
probably brought home embroidered textiles from the
Middle Eastern countries after the Crusades, and the
trade and spice routes carried not only articles for sale
but also itinerant craftsmen, who practised their skills
wherever they settled. The spread of cross stitch designs from their place of origin to so many different
locations makes it difficult to identify any one cross
stitch design as having originated in any particular
region. Even today, it is fascinating to note the same
motifs occurring in the traditional peasant embroideries
of countries as far apart, geographically, as Russia and
Mexico.

THE ENGLISH TRADITION

The earliest reference to embroidery in England occurs
in a document dating from 679 AD. During the following
centuries, embroidery enriched ceremonial vestments
belonging both to Church and royalty, and it is probable
that domestic versions existed but have not survived.
There is, however, little evidence in Europe of the use
of cross stitch or its variations before the sixteenth century, with the exception of the badge of the Knight's
Templar on the Syon Cope, now exhibited at the
Victoria and Albert Museum, London. Crossed stitches
began to be commonly used during the sixteenth century, worked on needlepoint hangings, table covers,
carpets and furniture coverings by the female house-
holds of the courts and castles.

During this period, embroidery was worked either in
home-produced woollen threads or silk imported from
the Middle East. A linen fabric known as 'canvas' was
used as the background and cross stitch was often
worked together with tent stitch and satin stitch. Some
stitches, such as the double running or Holbein stitch
used to outline cross stitch areas, are thought to have
been introduced to England by Catherine of Aragon,
the first wife of Henry VIII. Embroidery designs were
copied from a number of sources, including woven
tapestry hangings, herbals and gardening books.
Jacques Le Moyne's *La Clef des Champs*, published in
1586, is often quoted as an influential design source.
Many examples of fine stitching were recorded in the
contemporary portraits of that period.

Throughout the sixteenth century, furniture was
heavy and rather uncomfortable, and padded cushions
helped to provide welcome comfort and warmth in the
home. Inventories throughout this period show that
embroidered cushions were used in both great and
humble houses. An inventory drawn up in 1523 lists
cushions covered with 'velvet of divers colours imbrodered with golde' and 'tawny sarcenet imbrodered
with branchis'.

Sixteenth century embroiderers stitched emblematic
designs in addition to the stylized floral patterns from
the design books. These abstract motifs were usually
copied from pieces of embroidered fabric which had
been brought into England from other parts of Europe,
or from further afield. Queen Elizabeth I was reputedly
a fine needlewoman, as was Mary Queen of Scots who
filled the months of her captivity producing exquisite
examples of embroidery, often using cross stitch, some

of which survive today.

After the restoration of the monarchy in 1660, domestic life in Britain became more comfortable. Women embroidered many more decorative items than before, including pictures and firescreens which often featured realistic biblical scenes. As travel and trade increased, voyagers returned from the Far East and the Americas bringing new design sources which could be utilized. Strange foreign flowers, beasts and birds found their way into traditional embroidery patterns. When adapted for cross stitch, the designs often lost much of their original form and became merely decorative details.

By the middle of the eighteenth century, many of the great houses of the land had 'needlework rooms' where large panels of needlepoint and tapestry were mounted on the walls, framed by elaborately carved mouldings. However, after that time the popularity of embroidery and needlepoint seems to have declined a little, probably due to changes of fashion in home furnishings. When printed fabrics became available in large quantities, people were provided with a cheap alternative to heavy tapestries and needlepoint panels.

The British middle classes were beginning to enjoy increasing wealth during the early part of the nineteenth century. This prosperity was mainly due to large profits from industrialization, and the middle classes soon began to share the leisure pursuits which had previously been the prerogative of the upper classes. From the 1850s onwards, most middle class women and young girls spent a great deal of time doing embroidery and 'fancy work' (crafts like crochet, tatting and macramé). Their houses were full of decorated cushions, mats, pictures, antimacassars, doyleys, and other articles worked from patterns in the growing number of weekly women's magazines. These items were generally displayed in the main rooms, purely as decoration and as a way of showing off the skills of the ladies of the house. Cross stitch was still used, but mainly for sampler stitching until interest in a type of cross stitch embroidery known as 'Berlin woolwork' spread throughout Europe and America.

SAMPLERS

Personal collections of stitches and designs have been embroidered for hundreds of years by both women and children. These collections are called samplers (from the Old French 'essamplaire', meaning a pattern which

could be copied) and many have survived to the present day, forming a unique record of domestic needlework from the fifteenth to the twentieth century. Samplers were worked primarily as a learning process to try out different stitches, techniques and designs which could then be used as reference material. The designs were probably copied by one person and then passed on to someone else, so many of the samplers show similar designs worked in different ways. The earliest reference occurs in 1502, when the account book of Elizabeth of York showed the purchase of 'lynnyn cloth for a sampler'.

Early samplers show realistic and fanciful flowers, fruit, animals, birds and figures as well as border patterns, and many of the designs were copied from printed pattern books. The samplers were worked on linen fabric or fine canvas using silk, linen or wool threads and used a variety of stitches and techniques including cross stitch, cut and drawn thread work and metal thread embroidery. Later samplers, particularly those from the eighteenth and nineteenth centuries, are worked mainly in cross stitch and show an increasing use of alphabets and religious texts.

During the nineteeth century, the majority of samplers were stitched by children in schools and orphanages as part of their general education. Embroidered samplers were based on the alphabet to give pupils a thorough grounding in the sequence of letters, spelling and also in practical embroidery skills. After leaving school, many girls went into domestic service, and to have a good standard of spelling and needlework meant that they could hope to avoid menial kitchen work and perhaps become a lady's maid. A lady's maid would spend much of her time repairing garments and marking the household linen with embroidered names and monograms, so neat stitching and accurate spelling was essential.

Girls usually worked one complete alphabet sampler each year during their schooldays and, in most schools, the teacher also kept a needlework exercise book and

CROSS STITCH EMBROIDERY is a perennially popular way of decorating items of household linen. During the 1920s and '30s, transfer-printed designs were widely available, often in kit form.

carefully recorded the progress of her pupils. Many of these books have survived intact and show examples of each child's work stitched or pinned to the pages. In addition to embroidery, small samples of knitting, crochet, patchwork and plain sewing were included. A typical book of this kind was worked by pupils of the Westbourne Union School, Sussex during the period 1842 to 1844. Each page of work is headed by a strip of canvas showing the girl's name and age worked in cross stitch.

Most nineteenth century samplers contain one or two simple alphabets and sets of numerals enclosed within a narrow border. The stitches are usually worked in coloured cross stitch on coarse woollen fabric or occasionally on linen. Ordinary cross stitch and marking cross stitch are usually the only stitches used on this type of sampler. The date of completion and the christian name and surname of the stitcher and her age were usually added. Complex monochrome samplers were also produced, usually by girls living in orphanages, some containing as many as twenty alphabets, moral verses, religious texts and motifs of houses, animals and flowers.

Sampler texts tended to be sombre and worthy. A sampler completed in 1883 shows a tiny bible surrounded by the words 'Behold the BOOK whose leaves display JESUS the life the truth the way'. Inscriptions on other samplers include 'God is love abide with us time is short' and 'Remember thy Father and Mother in the days of thy youth'. On some samplers, the wording is a little more human – one mid-Victorian example reveals 'here a figure there a letter one done bad another better'.

As well as embroidery, plain sewing was taught in schools. An educational manual *Plain needlework in all its branches,* published in 1849 for use in the National Industrial School of the Holy Trinity at Finchley, London, states the need for all women to have 'a practical acquaintance with needlework . . . this is more particularly the case with reference to females in humble life, whether with a view to domestic neatness and economy, or to profitable occupation in a pecuniary light'. The manual lists twelve basic stitches including cross stitch, buttonhole stitch and herringbone stitch. Sewing samplers were worked on white linen or cotton and illustrate the range of techniques used to create the garments and household linen of the day. The fabric was first hemmed, then cut and darned. Buttonholes, covered buttons, hooks, eyes and fabric tags and tapes

were added as well as types of seams and shaping techniques, such as tucks and gathers. These samplers often show exquisite workmanship and many include decorative stitching, such as names and dates, worked in cross stitch or chain stitch.

BERLIN WOOLWORK

Berlin woolwork was a type of cross stitch embroidery which first appeared in Berlin during the 1830s. It was worked on canvas using a great variety of different coloured woollen threads. The designs were printed in chart form on squared paper, with one square representing one stitch. By counting the squares and stitching them with the correct shades of thread, the needlewomen could copy the designs accurately. Berlin woolwork was used extensively for pictures and to cover cushions, chair seats and stools as well as to make small items like slippers, pincushions and purses. Three-dimensional areas were produced by the use of a textured stitch called velvet stitch. Portions of the design were closely worked in this stitch and the resulting pile trimmed with scissors to give an almost sculptured effect.

The charts were originally printed in black line on white paper and laboriously hand coloured, but as the craze swept through Europe and America, later charts were printed in full colour to keep up with the demand. quantities from 1831 by Mr Wilks, the owner of a prestigious needlework shop at 186 Regent Street, London. By the 1840s, at least 14,000 different patterns for Berlin woolwork had been published and, by 1844, Mr Wilks was able to advertise his shop as having the 'largest and best assorted stock in the Kingdom'.

Special woollen threads were spun for woolwork and these took a faster, more brilliant dye than the worsted threads which had previously been used for embroidery. The threads were manufactured at Gotha in Germany and dyed in Berlin. They had a soft, silky finish and were called 'Berlin wool' or 'Zephyr yarn'. With the introduction of aniline dyes in the 1850s, the colours became more brilliant and rather gaudy. Berlin woolwork was usually worked on white cotton 'German' canvas, as this was extremely hardwearing and every tenth thread was coloured yellow to aid counting.

Floral designs were particularly popular for woolwork articles. Floral garlands and bouquets were usually worked against a light-coloured background. Early designs of passion flowers, roses, pansies, auriculas and other small blooms look delicate and almost lifelike but, by about 1860, exotic flowering plants like fuchsias, arum lilies and hothouse orchids were used in profusion, usually worked on a black background.

As the craze for Berlin woolwork increased, the designs became more florid and crude, and the embroidered results looked garish. Extremely bright colours were used for the designs, with detailed, naturalistic shading on the petals and leaves. Other favourite subjects of the period were birds and animals, particularly parrots and macaws. Copies of sentimental paintings by some of the eminent artists of the day, including Sir Edwin Landseer, were also popular subjects. In America, there was a craze for portraiture worked in Berlin woolwork, particularly depicting George Washington and Benjamin Franklin, whose features graced cushion covers and pictures by the thousand. Highlights of silk thread and glass beads were often added to the portraits, creating the effect of light and shade.

During the 1860s and 1870s, naturalistic designs gradually declined in popularity and were replaced by ornamental and geometric patterns, such as Greek key borders, scrolls and arabesques. The women's magazines of the period reflected this trend and *The Young Ladies' Journal* of 1864 contained many charts for geometric borders. The magazine's editorial states that 'We continue to supply our readers with as many designs in strips and borders in Berlin work as possible because we are assured of their utility. It is quite easy to be working these strips . . . when worked

CROSS STITCH is found on traditional embroideries in many diverse cultures throughout the world. In these examples from Thailand, cross stitch is worked alongside satin stitch and hand appliqué.

they may be used for so many purposes – cushions, stools, borders of table-covers and travelling bags, etc.'

THE LAST HUNDRED YEARS

By the mid 1880s, the popularity of Berlin woolwork was declining, both in Europe and America. Gradually the florid, brightly-coloured woolwork designs began to be replaced by designs based on the study of ancient and ethnic textiles. The Royal School of Needlework was founded in London in 1872, with the twin aims of improving the general standard of embroidery and design and also to provide employment for women with needlecraft skills. The commissions undertaken by these women showed a high standard of technical excellence, and the results were especially pleasing when the designs were the work of leading artists and illustrators of the period, such as William Morris and Walter Crane. The RSN gave classes in embroidery techniques and the ladies in their workshops repaired and restored old textile pieces of value and special interest.

In 1876, the RSN exhibited some of its specially commissioned 'art needlework' at the Centennial Exposition in Philadelphia. The innovative designs and technical skill of these exhibits was influential in reviving interest in embroidery. Candace Wheeler, an American fabric designer, and Louis Tiffany, a leader of the American Art Nouveau movement, founded the Society for Decorative Arts in New York, which helped raise and revitalize the standards of American design and crafts-

manship within a wide range of crafts.

The study of old embroideries has uncovered a rich source of embroidery stitches and designs. As transport to foreign countries became safer, more comfortable and less expensive, more women began to travel abroad. They often brought back pieces of folk art embroidery, especially from Eastern Europe, Italy, India and the Aegean, which they studied and eventually copied. In 1920, the Embroiderers' Guild was formed and its first president, Louisa Pesel, did much to popularize traditional embroidery stitches such as cross stitch, pattern darning and double running stitch. Miss Pesel encouraged Guild members to take an active interest in using traditional designs and motifs from both historical and ethnic sources. Her research amongst the textiles in museum and private collections brought to light a wide range of lovely and forgotten cross stitch designs. Many of these were published in book form during the 1930s and are still in use today.

Hand embroidery remained a popular pursuit for many women throughout the first half of the twentieth century, together with crochet and hand knitting, and enjoyably filled many hours of spare time at home before the age of television. Many of the attractive pictures and pieces of table linen which survive from the twenties and thirties were probably bought in kit form from catalogues and draper's shops. The kits contained linen or cotton fabric printed with a design ready to be stitched using the supplied threads. Cross stitch designs of the period varied from multi-coloured, naturalistic patterns and folk art borders, through to abstract designs showing a strong Art Deco influence. Transfers for cross stitch could be bought without fabric and threads, or were given away free with the popular women's magazines of the day to boost their circulation. The design was printed on the transfer paper with a waxy ink, and was transferred to the fabric at home by pressing the wrong side of the transfer with a hot iron. The most elaborate pieces were much prized, often remaining unused for several generations, and have become treasured articles passed down through the family from mother to daughters, taking on the status of family heirlooms.

CROSS STITCH DESIGNS from India are usually spaced by eye, rather than by counting fabric threads. The colours and designs are delightfully exuberant, reflecting both Eastern and Western influences.

Interior design styles changed radically during the post-war years and there was no place for old-fashioned, elaborately embroidered home furnishings. The restrained Scandinavian styles of embroidery, such as Hardanger work and geometric designs in cross stitch, were much in demand during this period.

The late sixties and early seventies heralded a growing awareness of natural and ethnic designs, and this was reflected in both interior decoration and fashion. Inexpensive foreign holidays encouraged more people to travel abroad and many of them brought back garments and furnishings decorated with peasant embroidery. Today, with leisure time increasing, more and more men and women have begun to enjoy the craft and skills of cross stitch embroidery.

CROSS STITCH ROUND THE WORLD

Cross stitch has been used to decorate fabric in almost every part of the world, from Eastern Europe to Thailand; from Russia to Morocco. Designs and stitches have been exchanged between so many different cultures and geographical areas, through travel, trade and the availability of printed design books, that many design elements are now common to several cultures. However, there are many regional variations of similar cross stitch shapes, for example star, heart, flower and animal motifs.

One of the most important and widespread functions of cross stitch has been to ornament peasant garments and household linens, often as a means of indicating family wealth and status. Peasant embroidery is a purely domestic skill which is passed down through the generations from mother to daughter. The stitches are simple to work and the materials readily available. The thread colours were often limited, although these would be brilliantly dyed, often with the addition of brown or black for outlines. In China, cross stitch was almost always worked in dark blue thread on white fabric. Embroideries stitched in just one or two colours are perhaps the most striking of all and show off a complicated design to best advantage.

Complex and closely worked border patterns were actually created in the simplest way. Motifs used on their own are uncommon in peasant embroidery; instead they are usually repeated to form straight bands, which are then arranged one above another. Traditional Greek designs have as many as six or seven put together to form an intricate border, which is usually finished with a pattern that creates a broken outer edge.

CHAPTER TWO

PRACTICAL SKILLS

INTRODUCTION

Cross stitch embroidery is easy to work, even for the inexperienced stitcher, and you will quickly become confident working complicated designs in many colours of thread. For all but the smallest designs, stretch your fabric in a hoop or frame, since this will help you to stitch evenly and accurately.

Quantities are not given for each project. Instead, there are details of how to measure up and calculate your own fabric requirements. Estimate the amount of thread required by using one complete skein of each colour and measuring how much of the design is completed. The small projects use less than one skein of each colour, and are the ideal way to use up oddments.

If you are left-handed, many of the diagrams will be easier to follow if you prop the book up in front of a mirror, then follow the reflected images.

CHOOSING FABRIC, THREADS AND NEEDLES

An evenweave fabric is the best choice for cross stitch embroidery since it has the same number of identical threads to every 2.5 cm (1 in) of fabric. This number is called the count, or gauge, and the threads are counted so that stitches can be worked accurately from a chart. The most popular type of evenweave for cross stitch embroidery has groups of threads woven together to produce distinct blocks over which the stitches are worked. These fabrics, called Aida, Ainring, Hardanger and Binca, come in different counts and in a good colour range including pastels and bright colours.

All the projects in this book have been stitched with stranded cotton. This is the most versatile embroidery thread, being made from six loosely twisted strands so that a length can be split into different weights.

Use your threads in 38 cm (15 in) lengths to avoid tangling and fraying. Divide each skein of thread into convenient lengths by cutting a piece of stiff card 38 cm (15 in) long, winding the thread round and round its length, then cutting across the thread at each end. Make a plait from the cut lengths and remove each length as required by pulling one end gently from the plait.

Tapestry needles are ideal for use with evenweave fabric, since the blunt point separates the fabric threads without splitting them. They are available in sizes 14 to 26, graded from coarse (low numbers) to fine (high numbers).

THREADING THE NEEDLE

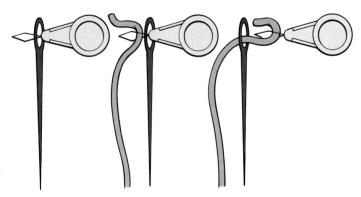

USING A NEEDLE THREADER This is a small metal or plastic gadget with a wire loop at one end. Pass the loop through the needle eye, place the end of the thread in the loop and draw both loop and thread through the eye.

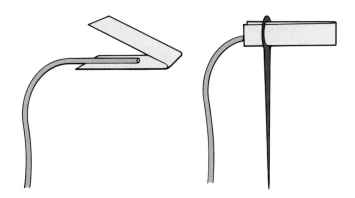

USING A PAPER STRIP Cut a 5 cm (2 in) long strip of thin paper narrow enough to pass through the needle eye. Fold the strip in half to enclose the end of the thread. Thread the paper through the needle eye, pulling the thread through at the same time.

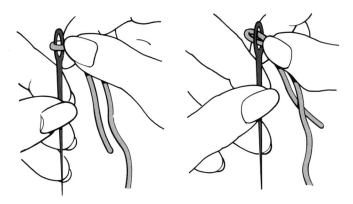

FOLDING THE THREAD Fold the end of the thread round the needle top and pull it tight. Slip the folded thread off the needle and push it through the needle eye.

STARTING AND FINISHING

Never tie a knot at the end of the thread. A knot can show through the finished piece of work and make an unsightly lump on the right side. A knot may also come undone during laundering, resulting in your stitching unravelling. Instead, secure the thread by making one or two tiny stitches in a space that will be covered by embroidery. Alternatively, leave about 5 cm (2 in) of thread hanging loose which can be darned in later.

When working an area which is partly stitched, secure the new thread neatly on the wrong side by sliding the needle under a group of stitches to anchor about 2.5 cm (1 in) of thread underneath them. To finish a length of thread, slide the needle under a group of stitches on the wrong side and cut off the loose end.

EMBROIDERY FRAMES

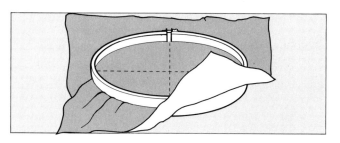

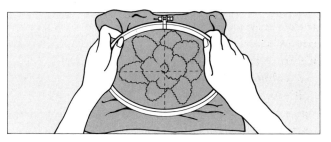

HOOPS

1 Embroidery hoops are available in various sizes and consist of two sections placed one inside the other. The fabric is sandwiched in-between and the sections are secured by a screw at the side.

4 Loosen the screw and remove the larger hoop at the end of every stitching session. Press the fabric down with your thumbs at the edges of the hoop, lifting the larger hoop at the same time.

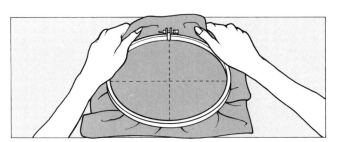

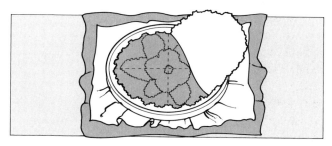

2 Spread the fabric, right side up, over the smaller hoop and press the larger hoop down over the top. Tighten the screw slightly until the larger hoop fits round the smaller hoop.

5 Protect your work by spreading tissue paper over the right side of the embroidery before it is remounted. Cut away the paper to expose the next area to be worked.

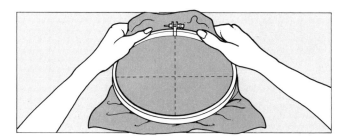

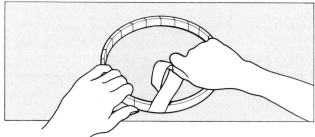

3 Manipulate the fabric with your fingers until it is evenly stretched, keeping the larger hoop pressed well down over the smaller hoop. Tighten the screw fully. Move the hoop along after one portion of the design is completed.

6 Bind the smaller hoop, without the screw, with thin cotton tape to help prevent the fabric working loose and sagging as you stitch. The tape will also help avoid damage to delicate fabrics.

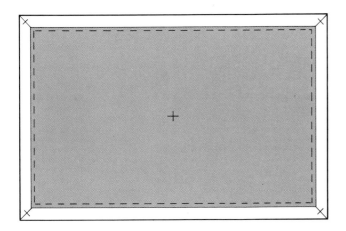

STRETCHER This is a simple, non-adjustable frame made from four pieces of wood joined at the corners. Mark the centre of each side of the frame and the centre of each edge of the fabric. Working outwards from the centre of one side of the frame, line up the marks and attach the fabric to this side with drawing pins or staples. Repeat on the opposite side, making sure the fabric grain is straight, then attach the fabric to the other two sides in the same way.

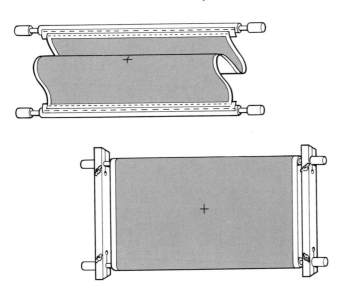

ROTATING FRAME

1 Attach the top and bottom of the fabric to the webbing on both the rollers following the instructions given for a slate frame. Loosen the wing nuts on the side pieces and slot in the rollers, taking up any slack in the fabric by winding it round one of the rollers.

2 Turn the rollers to stretch the fabric and tighten the nuts firmly on the side pieces. Lace the fabric to the frame as for a slate frame. You may need to make several adjustments to get the tension even over the whole surface of the fabric. Slacken off the tension of the lacing between embroidery sessions.

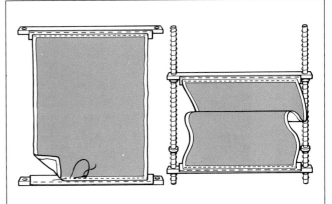

SLATE FRAME

1 Turn over and tack 1.5 cm (½ in) all round the fabric. Mark the centre of the webbing on the rods, also mark the centre of the top and bottom of the fabric. Line up the marks and stitch the fabric to the webbing with back stitch (page 22), working from the centre point outwards. Use a strong thread such as buttonhole thread.

2 Screw two nuts onto each side arm and move them to the centre. Slot the top of the side arms into the holes in the top rod, then repeat at the bottom. When using a piece of fabric longer than the side arms, first roll the excess round one of the rods.

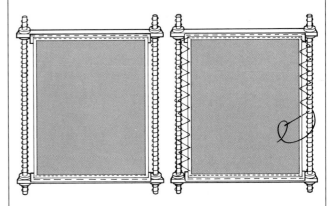

3 Push the rods along the side arms so that the fabric is pulled taut, then move the nuts close to the rods and screw a locking nut on to each end of the side arms. Tighten all the nuts in turn so that the fabric is evenly stretched.

4 Lace the sides of the fabric to the sides of the frame with buttonhole thread, leaving a length of thread free at top and bottom. Tighten the lacing from the centre outwards, working alternately along each side to tension the fabric evenly. Secure the thread ends by knotting them round the frame. Slacken off the tension between embroidery sessions.

EACH COLOURED square represents one stitch to be worked over one or more woven blocks of fabric. The instructions for each project – either in the main body of text or the captions – specify the number of fabric blocks.

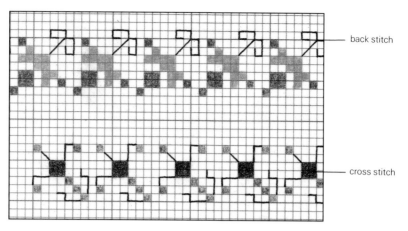

back stitch

cross stitch

WORKING FROM A CHART

Read the instructions given with each project carefully before starting to stitch. They will tell you how to mark the exact position of the embroidery on the fabric, and at which point on the chart you should start from. Usually this is the centre, and you will need to mark your starting point on the chart with a pencil mark which can be erased later.

Beginning from the correct point and working outwards, embroider one stitch on the fabric for every coloured square shown on the chart. The instructions also tell you the number of woven fabric blocks you need to cover with each stitch so that the design will work out to the correct size.

USING WASTE CANVAS

This technique enables you to work counted cross stitch neatly and accurately on fabric which does not provide a natural grid for the stitching, due to its uneven weave. Canvas is a stiffened evenweave material normally used for needlepoint, but here it is temporarily attached to the fabric to provide a grid for the embroidery. You can buy special waste canvas which has coloured threads woven in at

intervals to make counting simpler, or you can use ordinary needlepoint canvas, providing the threads are not interlocked. The tulip bedlinen on page 38 is embroidered using waste canvas, and the technique will allow you to work any of the other designs in the book on fabric which is not evenly woven, including towelling and sweatshirt fabric.

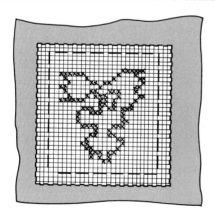

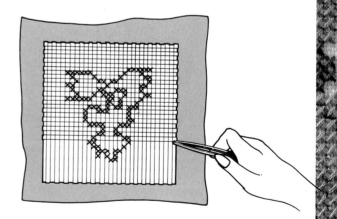

1   Choose canvas with the same count as the fabric suggested in the project instructions. Tack a piece of canvas onto the right side of the fabric, making sure it is large enough to allow the complete design to be worked. Work the cross stitch design over the canvas grid, taking the stitching through both canvas and fabric.

2   Remove the tacking and cut away the canvas close to the design. Pull out the canvas threads individually with tweezers, starting from one corner and pulling out all the threads which lie in one direction first. It may help to first moisten the canvas with water. Pull out the remaining threads.

BASIC STITCHES

These are the basic stitches used in cross stitch embroidery, plus a knotted stitch you can use to add areas of texture. There are also two reversible variations of ordinary cross stitch which you may prefer to use when both sides of the fabric you are embroidering may be seen. These stitches are particularly useful when embroidering household linen with names or monograms.

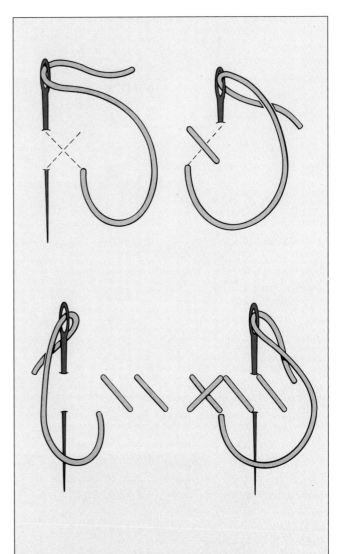

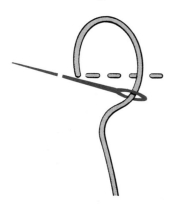

RUNNING STITCH Use to work design lines for a lighter effect than back stitch (below), and to decorate a hem. The stitches and spaces should be of identical length. Pass the needle through the fabric at regular intervals with an 'in-and-out' movement.

BACK STITCH Back stitch makes a solid, slightly raised line. Use it for working design lines and also to finish off hems. This stitch makes the foundation row for whipped back stitch (below).

Work back stitch from right to left, making small, even stitches forwards and backwards along the row, as shown in the diagram. Keep the stitches of identical size.

WHIPPED BACK STITCH

Whipped back stitch makes a heavier, more raised line than the previous stitch, and it looks attractive worked in two colours round a hem.

First, work a foundation row of back stitch (above). Using a second thread, whip over this line from right to left, as shown, using a tapestry needle to avoid picking up the fabric threads.

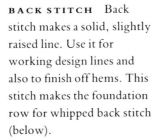

CROSS STITCH There are several methods of working cross stitch although the top diagonal stitches should always slant in the same direction, usually from bottom left to top right. When a variation of light and shade across the embroidered surface is required, vary the directions of the stitches so that they catch the light.

The first two diagrams show cross stitch worked individually. This method produces slightly raised crosses and you should complete each cross before proceeding to the next one. Work small details and individual stitches on the designs in this way.

To cover larger areas, work each row of cross stitch over two journeys. First, work a row of diagonal stitches from right to left, then complete the crosses with a second row of diagonal stitches worked in the opposite direction. If you work a single row of diagonal stitches, it is then called half cross stitch.

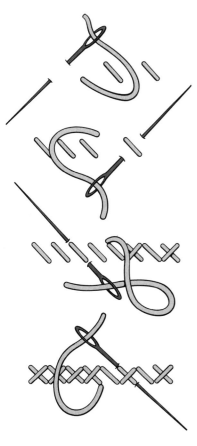

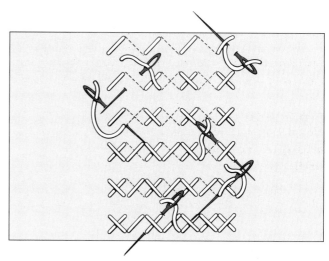

ALTERNATE CROSS STITCH This looks the same on the right side of the fabric as ordinary cross stitch (page 22) does when it is worked over two journeys. This method ensures a perfectly even stitch tension although it uses considerably more thread than the previous methods, being worked over four journeys.

On the first journey, from right to left, work every alternate diagonal stitch along the row. Complete the diagonals on the second journey, working from left to right. Next, cross these stitches by working the top row of diagonals on two more journeys.

MARKING CROSS STITCH Marking cross stitch is a reversible variation of ordinary cross stitch (page 22), with each stitch forming a cross on the front of the fabric and a square of straight stitches on the reverse. It is useful for working lettering and monograms on clothing and household linen, but note that some of the stitches have to be re-crossed in order to make complete squares on the reverse.

Follow the sequence of stitches shown in the diagram. The straight stitches formed on the back of the fabric are shown next to each stitch. You may need to make further re-crosses, especially when working lettering, in order to complete every square.

TWO-SIDED CROSS STITCH Two-sided cross stitch makes an identical stitch on both sides of the fabric and has the same uses as the previous stitch. Each row is worked over four journeys and you must always remember to make the two half stitches at the beginning of both the second and fourth row.

Begin at the left-hand side, working every alternate diagonal stitch along the row. Then make an extra half stitch on the right-hand side before returning along the line to complete the alternate crosses. On the third journey, work the missing diagonals from left to right. Turn, then work another half stitch, as shown, and complete the cross stitches on the fourth journey from right to left. When working lettering, you may need to stitch over a cross stitch so that you can continue the row. Do this neatly and take care to secure the thread ends under an existing stitch.

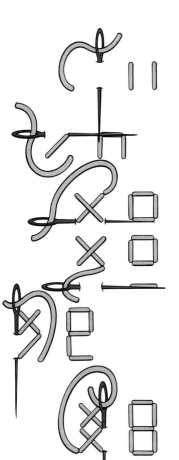

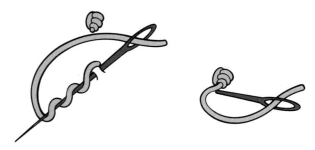

FRENCH KNOT Use French knots to add texture to flat expanses of cross stitch and also to work raised details, such as flower centres and tiny berries. Try working this stitch with three or four contrasting threads in the needle.

Bring the thread through the fabric and hold it taut with the left hand. Twist the needle round the thread several times, then tighten the twists. Still holding the thread in the left hand, turn the needle round and insert it in the fabric close to the point where it originally emerged. Pull the thread through the twists to the back of the fabric.

EXPERIMENTAL STITCHES

All the stitches shown in this section have a square format and can be used instead of cross stitch to work the designs shown in the pattern libraries. Use the diagrams in conjunction with the Experimenting chapter beginning on page 140, and remember that the first stitch works best on fabric, and the following seven are for use on needlepoint canvas.

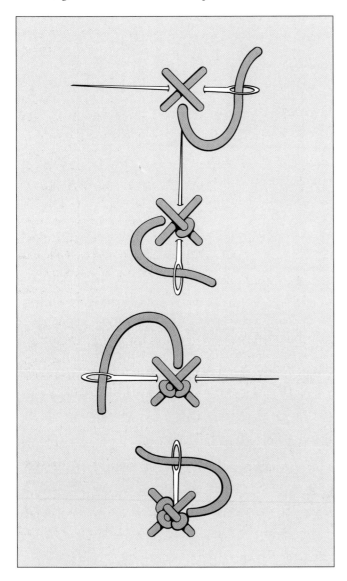

SQUARE BOSS This stitch makes square, raised knots which look good contrasted with ordinary cross stitch (page 22) of the same size.

First, work an ordinary cross stitch. Then, starting at the bottom right of this cross, cover each arm with a back stitch (page 22) worked through the fabric. You can use two colours of thread by working all the cross stitches on one journey and the back stitches on a second journey.

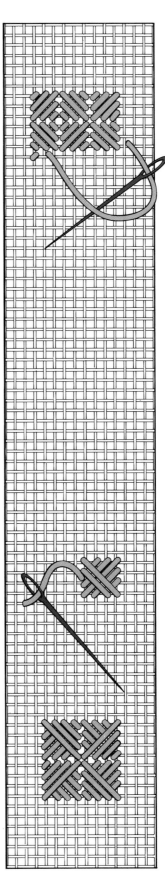

REVERSED CUSHION STITCH Reversed cushion stitch makes a neat pattern of regular blocks with the varying slant of the stitches producing an attractive light and shade effect. You can shade this stitch by using several close shades of one colour over a large area.

Each reversed cushion stitch block consists of five diagonal stitches of graduated length worked over a square of three canvas threads. Arrange the blocks in horizontal rows and reverse the slant of the stitches on alternate blocks.

CROSSED CORNERS CUSHION STITCH Crossed corners cushion stitch covers the canvas well and makes an interesting pattern, highlighted by the light and shade effect created by the varying direction of the stitches.

First, work seven diagonal stitches of graduated length to cover a square of four canvas threads. Then work four diagonal stitches over one half of the block, as shown in the diagram. Arrange the blocks in groups of four, as shown, or so that the overstitched corners meet and make a diamond shape.

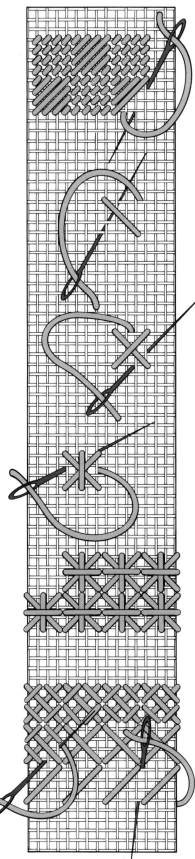

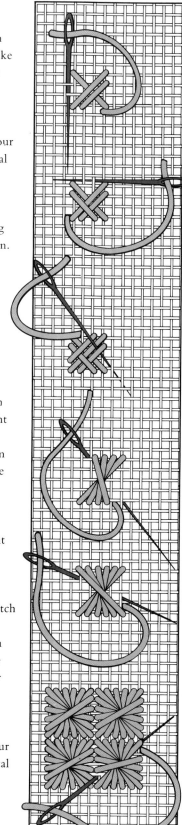

CHEQUER STITCH

Chequer stitch is often worked over large areas in one colour since it looks like brocade, but it can also be stitched in two colours to make an attractive chequerboard pattern.

Work the blocks over four vertical and four horizontal canvas threads. Alternate blocks of sixteen small diagonal stitches with blocks of seven graduating diagonal stitches, as shown.

LEVIATHAN STITCH

Leviathan stitch makes a pattern of raised blocks which can be worked in more than one colour of thread, giving a chequerboard effect.

Work leviathan stitch in horizontal rows from right to left, beginning at the lower edge. First, work an ordinary cross stitch (page 22) over four vertical and four horizontal canvas threads. Then work two stitches to form an upright cross of the same size directly over the top.

RICE STITCH

Rice stitch can be worked in two weights of thread, using a heavy thread for the large crosses and a finer one for the corner stitches.

Begin by covering the area with cross stitches (page 22) worked over four vertical and four horizontal canvas threads, then add small diagonal stitches across each corner.

WOVEN CROSS STITCH

Woven cross stitch has a textured, almost woven appearance and it can be worked in two contrasting or toning shades of thread to make a chequerboard pattern. A further colour contrast can be added by framing each stitch with back stitch (page 22).

Work the stitches in horizontal rows, starting at the lower edge. First, work an ordinary cross stitch (page 22) over four vertical and four horizontal canvas threads. Overstitch the cross with four diagonal stitches, which are woven over and under each other as they are worked. Follow the sequence of unders and overs shown in the diagram.

RHODES STITCH

Rhodes stitch makes a pattern of three-dimensional blocks and it can be worked over five, six or more canvas threads.

Work straight stitches across the block so that they follow each other in an anti-clockwise direction. Begin by working the first stitch from the bottom left-hand corner to the top right-hand corner. Continue in this way, filling every hole round the square. When working over an even number of threads, add a short vertical stitch spanning two threads at the centre of each block.

CHAPTER THREE

FLORAL
DESIGNS

INTRODUCTION

Floral and plant designs remain one of the most popular sources for all kinds of craftwork designs, particularly those intended for hand embroidery. The charm and freshness of cross stitch embroidery is perfectly complemented by a floral design, whether single blossom, spray or lavish bouquet.

Nature gives us a wonderful array of flowering plants, many species of which have been hybridised by plant breeders over the last century to delight us with larger, longer-lasting blooms in a range of sumptuous colours. The variety of flowers is almost endless: spring and summer flowering bulbs, border perennials, short-lived summer bedding plants, fragrant shrubs and trees which give year-round colour, aromatic herbs and house plants. Today, due to the increasing popularity of conservatory gardening, exotic species like orchids, tender tropical plants and fruiting shrubs are more widely grown by the amateur, and many plant varieties have been specially bred to flourish in the dry conditions created by central heating.

As well as traditional garden favourites, such as rambler roses and pansies, other cottage garden flowers would make lovely cross stitch designs. Many old-fashioned flowers have picturesque common names including love-lies-bleeding, forget-me-not, bleeding heart, leopard's bane, coral bells and cupid's dart. These interesting names can easily be incorporated into your design by embroidering them below the flowers using one of the small alphabets from the pattern library.

The projects in this chapter include several designs (gifts to treasure, page 37) which are quick and easy to stitch, even for the inexperienced needleperson. All these projects are small enough to be worked directly in the hand, without the need for an embroidery hoop, and they are ideal for using up any odds and ends of evenweave fabric and embroidery threads you may have. While working these small designs, your confidence will quickly grow as you gain valuable experience following a cross-stitch chart and executing the individual stitches. You will soon feel able to proceed to a more challenging design, perhaps the traycloth on page 40.

The larger, more complex projects, such as the apple blossom afternoon teacloth (page 31) and pansy picture (page 32), are embroidered in exactly the same way as the small items, working one stitch for every coloured square shown on the chart. Cross stitch can be worked on ready-made articles like bedlinen by attaching a temporary canvas grid known as waste canvas. The tulip designs on page 39 are worked by this method, but you may prefer to substitute one of the floral sprays shown in the colour and black and white pattern libraries. Included in these pages are charts for an all-over pattern which can be substituted for the trellis tie-back design on page 34, and a large spray of scarlet poppies which would make a stunning picture.

Always use an embroidery hoop or frame to hold your fabric taut when working all but the smallest designs. Although this may feel rather cumbersome at first, the benefits will be well worth the initial effort. Fabric stretched in a hoop or frame stays evenly stretched, and this allows the stitches to be worked quickly and accurately without the fabric weave becoming distorted and pulled out of shape. At the end of each embroidery session, slacken off the hoop to prevent permanent creasing of the fabric and store it wrapped in white tissue paper.

The pattern library at the end of this chapter illustrates many more easy-to-stitch designs featuring single flowerheads, small flowers and sprigs which can be used in various ways. You could, for example, work a series of tiny flowers to make an attractive set of napkins, then group several of the flowers together and embroider them at each corner of a coordinating tablecloth.

Also included in the pattern library are two designs for greetings cards. These are in the form of small rectangular frames decorated with flower motifs. The centre of each frame has been left blank for you to add your own message such as 'Happy Birthday' or 'Congratulations'. To use these designs, sketch out your chosen wording on a piece of graph paper using one of the back stitch or cross stitch alphabets shown on pages 94 and 160. Then transfer the frame design square-by-square onto the graph paper so that it surrounds your message. If necessary, adjust the four sides, making them shorter or longer, so that the frame accommodates the lettering comfortably. Colour in the frame and the lettering with felt pens or coloured pencils to make yourself a working chart before you begin stitching. You will find more details of how to make and adapt charts on pages 142–143 of the Experimenting chapter.

There are many sources of inspiration for those stitchers who like to sketch and create their own designs. Flowers and plants are all around us, even when we live in a home without a garden. The countryside, even in these days of intensive agriculture, is still home to hundreds of flowering plants, while towns and cities boast parks with formal beds, flowering trees and shrubberies. You may be lucky enough to live close to a botanical garden or stately home, and can visit these for inspiration. Do not forget that a humble bunch of spring flowers or group of house plants can often provide the starting point for a glorious design.

If you do not feel capable of drawing a flower or plant from life, you will feel more confident finding a two-dimensional source to trace off and adapt into a cross stitch design. Specialist gardening magazines and seed catalogues are the most obvious sources of floral designs, but many others which can also spark off ideas surround us in everyday life, including patterned dress and furnishing fabrics, floorcoverings, illustrated books, wallpaper and even magazine advertisements. For example, if you already have curtains made from furnishing fabric with a distinct floral pattern, you can trace off each flower motif and make a chart from the tracings. Embroider the motifs in cross stitch using thread colours to match your fabric, then make up the embroideries into totally unique cushion covers which will coordinate perfectly with your room's colour scheme.

Libraries, too, provide a wealth of designs, especially in books dealing with art and antiques. Naturalistic flowers have been an important element for painters of many different schools, particularly the Dutch 'genre' painters and those who belonged to the Pre-Raphaelite Brotherhood. The nineteenth-century Arts and Crafts Movement of both Britain and America used flower shapes to create distinctive patterns for decorating household objects, as did Tiffany on his beautiful stained-glass lamps and window panels. In France, Art Nouveau glass made by Daum, Gallé and Lalique was often decorated with flowers and twining plant forms. During the nineteenth and early twentieth centuries, designers employed by potteries producing, amongst others, Shelley, Royal Winton, Royal Stanley, Carltonware, Minton and Royal Doulton, created hundreds of designs to keep up with the demand for flower-patterned tea sets, vases, dinner services and washing sets.

APPLE BLOSSOM
AFTERNOON TEACLOTH

 Delicately shaded sprays of apple blossom linked by sections of striped ribbon border make this cloth the perfect background for an afternoon meal of delicious cakes and refreshing tea.

MATERIALS

- 130 cm (51 in) by 130 cm (51 in) wide white 18 count Damask Aida evenweave fabric (Zweigart E3239, colour 1)
- DMC stranded cotton in the following colours: pinks 3731, 3733; shaded pinks 62, 112; dark red 304; orange 740; greens 700, 704, 890, 954
- Tapestry needle size 24
- Tacking thread in a dark colour
- Matching sewing thread
- Sewing needle and pins
- Large embroidery hoop

WORKING THE EMROIDERY

1 Tack a vertical line through the centre of the fabric, taking care not to cross any vertical threads. Mark the central horizontal line in the same way. Along one side of the fabric, tack a guideline 32 cm (12½ in) from the raw edge.

2 Begin at the centre of this side, noting that the tacked line gives the position of the centre of each flower motif. Mount the fabric in the embroidery hoop (page 19) and work one border flower motif in cross stitch (page 22) from the chart, using four strands of thread in the needle throughout. Start stitching at the centre of the orange area and work outwards, remembering that each square on the chart represents one cross stitch worked over three vertical and three horizontal woven blocks of fabric. Outline the petals (dark red 304) and add leaf veins (green 890) in back stitch (page 22) using two strands of thread.

3 Working towards one corner of the fabric from the completed flower motif, embroider one repeat of the ribbon border in the same way, then embroider the corner flower motif. At this point, stop and check your embroidery thoroughly, making sure that the motifs are complete and that the centre of each flower falls along the tacked line.

4 Tack a guideline from the centre of the completed corner flower motif along the adjacent side of the fabric

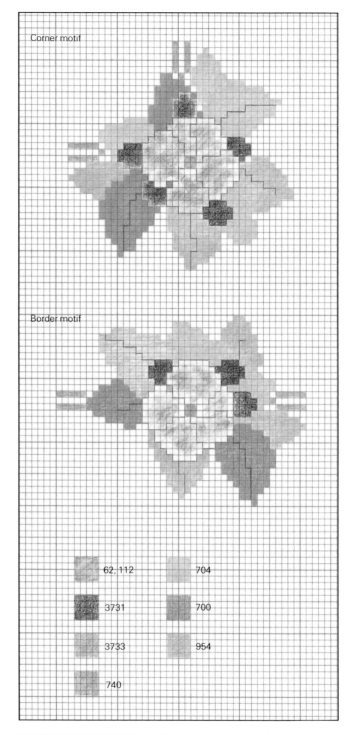

Corner motif

Border motif

	62, 112		704
	3731		700
	3733		954
	740		

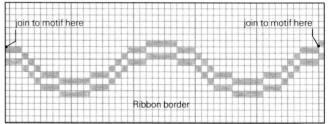

join to motif here   join to motif here

Ribbon border

EACH COLOURED square shown on the charts represents one cross stitch worked over three vertical and three horizontal woven blocks of fabric. The black lines indicate details worked in back stitch over three blocks.

towards the second corner. Work two repeats of the pink ribbon border and one border flower motif along this side. Work the second corner and repeat the process around the cloth.

MAKING UP THE CLOTH

1 Press the embroidery lightly on the wrong side.
2 Pin and tack a double 2.5 cm (1 in) hem (page 152) round the cloth and mitre the corners (page 153). Make sure that the embroidered border is an equal distance from the hem edge along each side of the cloth. Hand sew the hem (page 152).
3 To complete the cloth, work a row of spaced running stitches (page 22) round the cloth 2 cm (¾ in) from the edge in two strands of shaded pink 62.

EMBROIDER THIS charming, old-fashioned border of flowers and ribbon round the edge of your cloth, or just stitch the corner motifs for a simpler effect.

PANSY
PICTURE

 The pansy, or heartsease, is a widely-loved country garden flower and this picture will let you enjoy its colourful blooms all year round.

MATERIALS

- White 110 cm (43 in) wide 11 count Pearl Aida even-weave fabric (Zweigart E1007, colour 1)
- DMC stranded cotton in these colours: pinks 602, 892; mauves 340, 553; shaded mauve 126; purple 333; oranges 608, 741, 971; yellows 445, 726, 973; blue 826; shaded blue 91; greens 470, 704, 772, 912

- Tapestry needle size 24
- Tacking thread in a dark colour
- Stitch and tear embroidery backing (optional)
- Sewing needle
- Adjustable rectangular embroidery frame or rectangular wooden stretcher
- Sturdy cardboard
- Strong linen carpet thread or very fine string

MEASURING UP

The embroidered area measures approximately 20 cm (8 in) square. Add at least 10 cm (4 in) all round to allow for mounting the fabric in a frame while working the stitching, and to enable the finished embroidery to be laced round a piece of cardboard prior to framing.

THE NAME for the original wild pansy came from the French word 'pensée', meaning thought, and the plant has been given many other names over the centuries.

William Shakespeare wrote the following about the pansy – 'There is pansies, that's for thoughts'. You could add this phrase to the bottom of the picture using one of the small alphabets from the pattern library pages (pages 94 and 160). First work out the spacing of the letters on graph paper (page 143), then embroider them in cross stitch using three strands of thread.

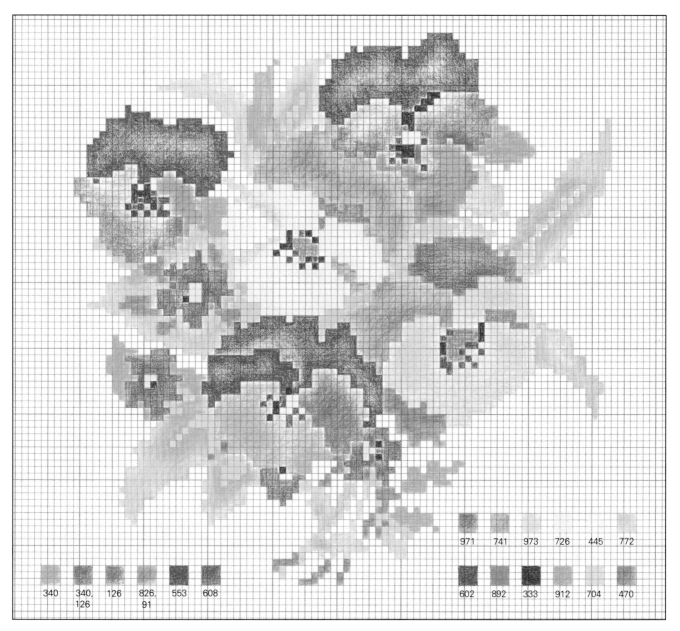

971 741 973 726 445 772

340 340, 126 826, 553 608
      126   91

602 892 333 912 704 470

PREPARING THE FABRIC

Cut out the fabric and tack a vertical line through the centre of the fabric, taking care not to cross any vertical threads. Mark the central horizontal line in the same way and mark the centre of the chart with a soft pencil. Mount the fabric in the frame or stretcher (page 20). If you are not very experienced at embroidery, tack a piece of stitch and tear embroidery backing on to the wrong side of the fabric to help prevent puckering.

WORKING THE EMBROIDERY

1 Begin by stitching at the centre of the design, noting that each coloured square on the chart represents one stitch worked over one woven block of fabric. Work in cross stitch (page 22) from the chart using three strands of thread throughout.

2 Some petals are stitched in a mixture of solid and shaded threads. To work these, use two strands of solid colour and one strand of shaded thread in the needle at the same time.

FINISHING THE PICTURE

Carefully tear away the embroidery backing close to the stitching, if used. Press the embroidery lightly on the wrong side with a warm iron. Follow the suggestions given on page 157 for framing.

TRELLIS
TIE-BACKS

 Show off pretty cotton curtains by adding a pair of shaped, stiffened tie-backs embroidered with this stylish trellis and flowers pattern. Four template sizes are given to accommodate curtains made in different widths.

MATERIALS

- Cream 130 cm (51 in) wide 18 count Ainring even-weave fabric (Zweigart E3793, colour 264)
- Cream cotton lining fabric
- DMC stranded cotton in the following colours: orange 971; yellow 444; greens 702, 704
- Tapestry needle size 24
- Tacking thread in a dark colour
- Matching sewing thread
- Sewing needle and pins
- Adjustable rectangular embroidery frame
- Double-sided self adhesive pelmet stiffener
- Dressmaker's pattern paper
- 4 brass D rings and 2 brass tie-back hooks

PREPARING THE FABRIC

Enlarge one of the templates on page 157 to the required size, draw twice onto dressmaker's pattern paper and cut out. Lay both pattern pieces on the right side of the evenweave fabric and mark the areas to be embroidered by tacking round the outside of the patterns, 1 cm (½ in) away from the edge of the paper.

WORKING THE EMBROIDERY

1 Tack a vertical line through the centre of each tacked shape, taking care not to cross any vertical threads. Mark the central horizontal line in the same way. Mount the fabric in the embroidery frame (page 20).

2 Beginning at the centre of one tacked shape, work the repeating green trellis pattern in cross stitch (page 22) from the chart, using three strands of thread in the needle throughout. Work outwards, remembering that each square on the chart represents one cross stitch worked over two vertical and two horizontal woven blocks of fabric, until the area inside the tacked lines is covered with trellis. Repeat the trellis pattern to cover the second shape.

3 Following the chart, work the flower motifs in alternate trellis squares in the same way as the trellis.

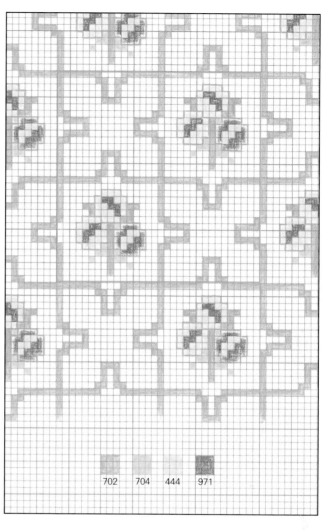

| 702 | 704 | 444 | 971 |

EMBROIDER THE *trellis and flowers pattern on to a cream or white background using colours which coordinate with your curtain fabric.*

EACH COLOURED *square shown on the chart represents one stitch worked over two vertical and two horizontal woven blocks of fabric.*

To complete the embroidery, outline each flower in back stitch (page 22), worked over two woven blocks of fabric, using two strands of thread.

MAKING UP THE TIE-BACKS

1 Remove the embroidery from the frame and press lightly on the wrong side over a well-padded surface. Use a warm iron and take care not to press too hard and crush the stitching.

2 Cut out the embroidered pieces, allowing a margin of 1 cm (½ in) of unworked fabric all round the design. Follow the illustrated steps on page 155 for making up the tie-backs.

GIFTS
TO TREASURE

 You are sure to enjoy embroidering these quick and easy designs and creating a wealth of special gifts to delight your family and friends. They are all small enough to be worked without a frame.

MATERIALS

BOOKMARK WITH BLUE FLOWERS: 30 cm (12 in) of 5 cm (2 in) wide cream evenweave 14 count embroidery tape with self-coloured woven border; DMC stranded cotton in the following colours: purple 333; blue 518; green 912

BOOKMARK WITH PINK FLOWERS: 30 cm (12 in) of 4.5 cm (1¾ in) wide white 14 count evenweave embroidery tape with contrasting woven border; DMC stranded cotton in the following colours: pink 604; green 561

OVAL PICTURE: 20 cm (8 in) square of white 11 count Pearl Aida evenweave fabric (Zweigart E1007, colour 1); DMC stranded cotton in the following colours: pink 603; purple 333; blues 796, 996; greens 906, 936
● White oval flexi hoop N3099

CIRCULAR PICTURE: 20 cm (8 in) square of white 11 count Pearl Aida evenweave fabric (Zweigart E1007, colour 1); DMC stranded cotton in the following colours: purple 333; orange 741; yellows 307, 743; blue 809; greens 912, 966; rust 920
● Woodgrain circular flexi hoop N3112

PAPERWEIGHT: 20 cm (8 in) square of white 11 count Pearl Aida evenweave fabric (Zweigart E1007, colour 1); DMC stranded cotton in the following colours: pinks 3607, 3609; shaded pink 62; mauves 553, 554; purple 333; yellow 444; greens 913, 936, 966
● Circular paperweight N857

PORCELAIN TRINKET BOX: 20 cm (8 in) square of cream 18 count Ainring evenweave fabric (Zweigart E3793, colour 264); DMC stranded cotton in the following colours: red 816, mauve 340, greens 563, 703
● Blue oval porcelain trinket box N852

JAM POT COVER: 30 cm (12 in) square of cream 18 count Ainring evenweave fabric (Zweigart E3793, colour 264); DMC stranded cotton in the following colours: pink 604; purple 333; turquoise 993; green 703; 90 cm (36 in) each of toning 1 cm (½ in) wide satin bias binding and 6 mm (¼ in) wide satin ribbon

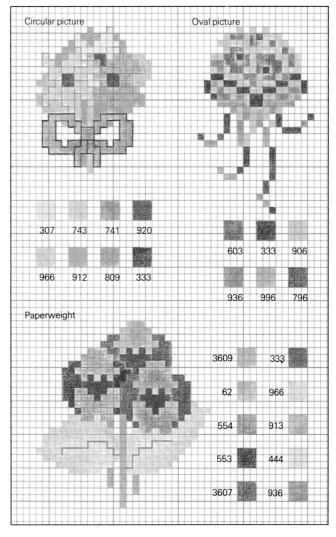

WORKING THE EMBROIDERIES

Fold each piece of fabric and tape in four, mark each centre with a pin, then mark the centre of each chart with a soft pencil. Work the designs from the centre outwards in cross stitch (page 22) from the charts, using three strands of thread in a size 24 tapestry needle.

MAKING UP THE GIFTS

Press the embroideries lightly on the wrong side. Finish the bookmarks by turning a 1 cm (½ in) double hem (page 152) at each end and hemming (page 152) in place. Mount the pictures in the flexi hoops and cut away surplus fabric. Follow the instructions supplied with the paperweight and trinket box. Cut away the fabric round the jam pot cover embroidery to leave a 20 cm (8 in) diameter circle. Bind the edge (page 154), place over the lid and secure with a rubber band. Tie the ribbon just below the lid and fasten in a bow.

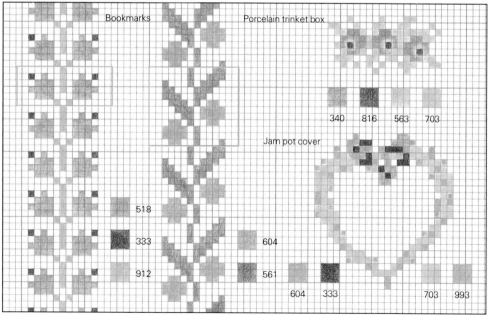

Bookmarks

Porcelain trinket box

| 340 | 816 | 563 | 703 |

Jam pot cover

518

333

912

604

561

604   333   703   993

FOR THE two bookmarks, porcelain trinket box and jam pot cover, work each cross stitch over two vertical and two horizontal woven blocks of fabric. For the two pictures and the paperweight, work each cross stitch over one vertical and one horizontal woven block.

TULIP
BEDLINEN

 Personalize plain, ready-made pillowcases and duvet cover with embroidered tulip motifs in two sizes. Stitched in shades of pink, green and blue to contrast with pale green fabric, this design uses the waste canvas technique, which enables counted thread stitches to be worked neatly on ordinary fabric. This useful technique is fully described and illustrated on page 21.

MATERIALS

- 2 ready-made pale green pillowcases and matching double duvet cover
- 68 cm (27 in) wide 10 count double thread waste canvas (Zweigart E510)
- DMC stranded cotton in the following colours: pinks 604, 962, 3607; blues 3755, 3760; greens 320, 701, 907
- Tapestry needle size 24
- Tacking thread in a dark colour
- Sewing needle and pins
- Matching sewing thread
- Embroidery hoop

PREPARING THE FABRIC

PILLOWCASE:
The small tulip design on the pillowcase is positioned near the open end. The design covers an area 27 squares wide and 29 squares deep and each coloured square represents one cross stitch worked over one vertical and one horizontal double canvas thread. Count out and cut a rectangle of waste canvas about 10 double threads larger all round than the design and mark the centre with a pin. Tack the canvas to the pillowcase, positioning it so that the centre of the design is 14 cm (5½ in) from both the open end and the top of the pillowcase. Mark the centre of the chart with a soft pencil.

DUVET COVER:
One large tulip design is used at each side of the duvet cover. To be able to work the embroidery comfortably, you first need to unpick the top seam and a short distance down each side seam. The design covers an area 39 squares wide and 46 squares deep and each coloured square represents one cross stitch worked over one vertical and one horizontal double canvas thread. Count out and cut two rectangles of waste canvas about

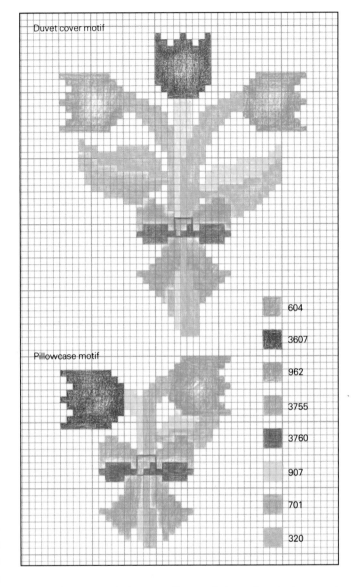

Duvet cover motif

Pillowcase motif

	604
	3607
	962
	3755
	3760
	907
	701
	320

10 double threads larger all round than the design, and mark the centres with pins. Tack one piece of canvas to each end of the top of the cover, positioning them so that the centre of the design is 23 cm (9 in) from the top seam and 30 cm (12 in) from the side seams. Mark the centre of the chart with a soft pencil.

WORKING THE EMBROIDERY

PILLOWCASE AND DUVET COVER:
1 Mount the fabric in the embroidery hoop (page 19), and work the design in cross stitch (page 22) from the chart, using three strands of thread in the needle throughout. Start stitching at the centre of the design and work outwards, remembering that each square on the chart represents one cross stitch worked over one vertical and one horizontal double thread of canvas.

USE THE *small tulip design to decorate a corner of each pillowcase and repeat the larger design at each side of the duvet cover. If you prefer to use a sheet and blankets, work one large motif at each side of the sheet, positioning them so that the embroidery will show when the top of the sheet is turned down over the blankets.*

THIS DESIGN *is worked by the waste canvas method, where a piece of canvas is tacked onto plain fabric to provide a grid for working cross stitch neatly and accurately. Each stitch is worked through both the canvas and the fabric, then the canvas threads are removed after all the embroidery has been completed.*

2 Following the chart, outline the centre of each bow in back stitch (page 22) using two strands of dark blue 3760 and working each back stitch over one, pair of canvas threads.

FINISHING THE BEDLINEN

1 Press the embroideries lightly on the wrong side over a well-padded surface. Use a warm iron and take care not to press too hard and crush the stitching.

2 Carefully follow the detailed illustrated instructions on page 21 for removing the waste canvas threads from the bed linen.

3 Turn the duvet inside out and re-stitch the top and side seams with matching thread. Turn the duvet right side out and give all the embroidered items a final light press.

SPRIGGED
TRAYCLOTH

 Make a traycloth into something special by decorating it with a colourful design of flower sprigs worked in one corner. Here, the embroidery has been designed to match the china, but it will complement other floral china just as well.

MATERIALS

- White 130 cm (51 in) wide 18 count Ainring even-weave fabric (Zweigart E3793, colour 1)
- DMC stranded cotton in the following colours: pinks 3731, 3733; red 304; orange 740; yellow 307; blues 798, 3755; greens 704, 954; brown 3021
- Tapestry needle size 24
- Tacking thread in a dark colour
- Sewing needle and pins
- Embroidery hoop

MEASURING UP

Measure the length and width of your tray and add at least 10 cm (4 in) extra all round to allow you to mount the design area comfortably in the embroidery hoop while stitching. Mark the finished size of the traycloth on the fabric with lines of tacking.

PREPARING THE FABRIC

On the chart, the design covers an area 49 squares wide and 39 squares deep, and each coloured square represents one stitch worked over two vertical and two horizontal woven blocks of fabric. Before you start to stitch, mark the position of the embroidery on the traycloth by marking out a rectangular area 98 blocks wide by 78 blocks deep with lines of tacking. Here, the embroidery is placed about 9 cm (3½ in) from the corner, but you may prefer to move it to a different position on the cloth.

WORKING THE EMBROIDERY

1 Tack a vertical line through the centre of the rectangle, taking care not to cross any vertical threads, then tack along the central horizontal line in the same way. Mark the centre of the chart with a soft pencil.
2 Mount the fabric in the embroidery hoop (page 19), and work the design in cross stitch (page 22) from the chart, using three strands of thread in the needle throughout. Begin stitching at the centre and work

outwards, remembering that each square on the chart represents one cross stitch worked over two vertical and two horizontal fabric blocks.

3 Outline the flower centres in back stitch (page 22) using two strands of thread.

MAKING UP THE TRAYCLOTH

1 Press the embroidery lightly on the wrong side.

2 Cut the fabric to the required size, allowing 2.5 cm (1 in) outside the tacked lines for the hem allowance.

3 Pin and tack a narrow double hem (page 152) round the traycloth, turning in the corners neatly and making sure that the hemline fold runs neatly between two rows of fabric blocks.

4 To complete the cloth, secure the hem with a row of back stitches worked close to the turned-over edge. Work each stitch over three or four woven blocks, using three strands of green 704. Press the hem edge lightly to make a crisp fold.

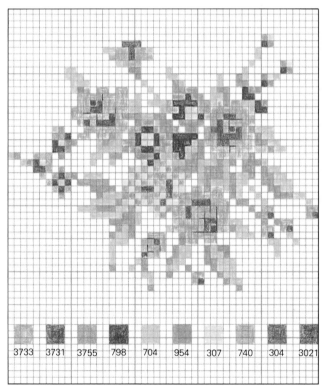

| 3733 | 3731 | 3755 | 798 | 704 | 954 | 307 | 740 | 304 | 3021 |

MAKE A SIMPLY prepared breakfast for one on a tray look really appetizing by serving it on a crisp white cloth embroidered with colourful flower sprigs.

Flower Sprigs and Frames

Sprigs and Bunches

Flowerheads and Jug of Flowers

Large Flowers

All-over Patterns and Borders

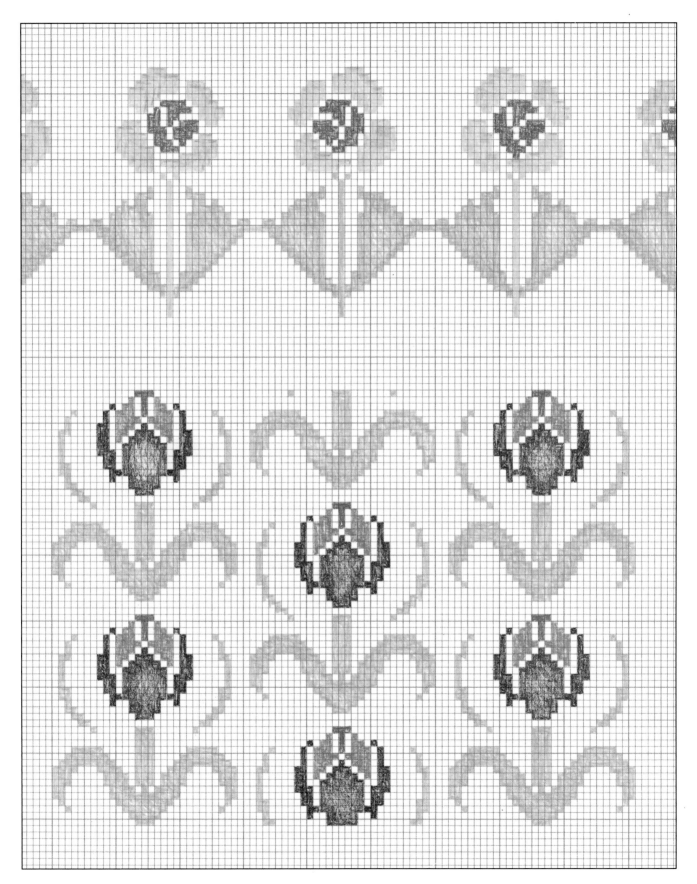

All-over Patterns and Borders

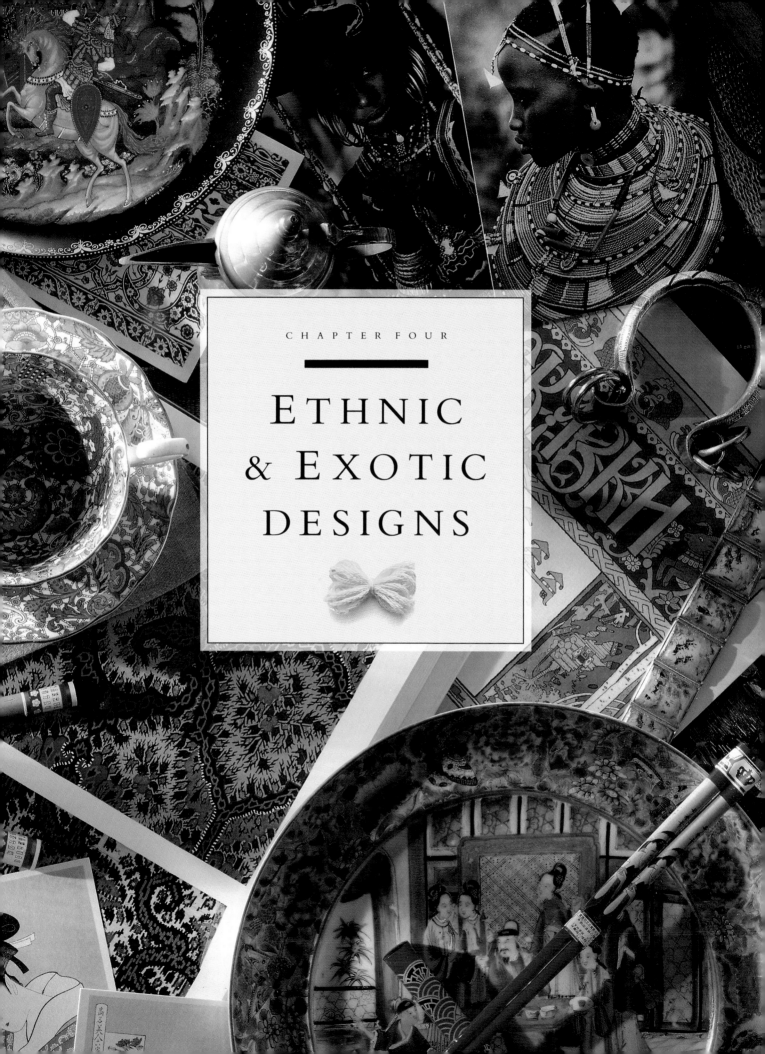

CHAPTER FOUR

ETHNIC & EXOTIC DESIGNS

INTRODUCTION

The theme of ethnic and exotic designs reflects a wide variety of cultures throughout the world; oriental influences from China and Japan, patterns from Europe and Scandinavia and designs from Africa and America have inspired the projects and the pattern library in this chapter.

Chinese and Japanese artforms have influenced Western design since these two countries were first visited by Western travellers. Their design heritage is rich and varied, from exquisitely embroidered silk robes and delicate porcelain to wood block prints and calligraphy.

The decoration on a pair of Royal Doulton stoneware vases was the original inspiration for the Chinese bluebirds of happiness picture on page 58. The vases date from the late 1920s or early 1930s, and the stylized bird pattern reflects the contemporary craze for all things Eastern. During the early twentieth century, oriental patterns were widely used to decorate pottery, dress and furnishing fabrics, furniture and wallcoverings.

One Chinese symbol is repeated across the background of the picture; it represents longevity, one of the Five Chinese Blessings, which also include peace and virtue. As well as the Five Blessings, the Chinese believe in Eight Precious Things – dignity, wealth, married happiness, harmony, charms against evil, charms against fire, personal charm and happiness. These are also represented by symbols, which were frequently used on ancient Chinese embroideries, particularly the rural cross stitch pieces, often hidden away in a border pattern. Living creatures also feature widely in Chinese folklore: the bat represents long life, the butterfly is the symbol of joy, summer and true love, while the dragon symbolizes goodness, strength and protection against evil.

The type of Japanese stitching which inspired the designs for the three scatter cushions on page 54 is called Sashiko quilting. It was originally worked through two layers of cotton fabric to make a thick, warm cloth suitable for winter garments. When garments began to wear out and appear shabby, further layers of fabric were added over the worn sections and re-quilted, often with a different design. Sashiko designs were always worked on indigo cotton fabric with white running stitches. The traditional designs were based on geometric shapes made up of straight lines, curves and circles, and they came from different regions of Japan. Here, the technique has been brought up to date and adapted for cross stitch embroidery, although it is still stitched in traditional white thread on dark blue fabric.

European folk art is a wonderful source of patterns and rich colour schemes. Germany, Austria, Italy and the countries of Eastern Europe such as Rumania, Hungary and Poland have a long and distinguished tradition of domestic decorative arts, including beautiful hand embroidery which is used to ornament garments and home furnishings. Many of the patterns in use today have been handed down from mother to daughter over countless generations. Typical folk art designs feature hearts, stars, crosses and other geometric patterns together with stylized representations of animals, birds and flowers including the carnation, tulip and rose. Sometimes just scarlet and black threads are used to contrast strongly with a white or pale cream background. But often, peasant designs are worked in a joyous riot of colours: scarlet, fuchsia pink, purple, royal blue, emerald green, turquoise and bright yellow can all be used on the same piece. The folk art place setting on page 60 uses a simple repeating pattern of stars and diamonds worked in strong colours.

The pattern library at the end of this chapter contains a further selection of borders for cross stitch inspired by

European folk art patterns. There are also several motifs on page 66 which can be used alone or framed by one of the borders. Transfer your design onto graph paper before you start to stitch, using a small mirror to help you work out a corner design for your chosen border. The illustration on page 144 shows you how to do this.

Also included in the pattern library is a group of designs inspired by the native Indian tribes of both North and South America. The symbols shown at the top of the page would be perfect for decorating the bib of a pair of children's dungarees or a toddler's playsuit. Embroider them directly onto the garment in bright, eye-catching colours using the waste canvas technique shown on page 21. Alternatively, you could embroider the designs on scraps of evenweave fabric and stitch these on to the garments to make decorative pockets or patches.

By contrast, twentieth-century Scandinavian designs have cool, clean and uncluttered lines. This restraint is echoed in the runner illustrated on page 52, with its simple pattern of blocks and lines worked in a subtle mix of colours. The design would look equally effective embroidered along each side of a tablecloth, or the pattern of blocks could be repeated in multiple rows to fill a cushion cover.

African patterns from woven textiles, beaded jewellery and mural paintings are bold and striking and often worked in hot, earthy colours. The design on the African bag, page 62, was taken from a mural painting adorning the mud walls of a Ndebele courtyard in the Central Transvaal region of South Africa. The mural design is repeated as a mirror-image across each wall. This bilateral symmetry is one of the strongest features of African mural painting in this area, and it is thought to echo the symmetrical structure of the human body.

The best project in this chapter to tackle if you are fairly new to embroidery is the folk art place setting on page 60. Here, a simple two-coloured border decorates the placemat and there is a small matching motif on the napkin. You may like to add interest and variety to your stitching by working each set of mat and napkin using two different thread colours, perhaps deep orange and green, or rust and dark gold, while keeping the same colour of fabric throughout. You will need to work with the fabric stretched in an embroidery hoop or adjustable frame to prevent uneven stitching and fabric distortion. Remember to slacken off the tension on the hoop or frame when you have finished stitching, and store your project wrapped in clean white tissue paper.

The larger projects like the Japanese cushions shown on page 54 and the Chinese bluebirds picture on page 58 probably look rather complicated and daunting to you unless you are an experienced stitcher. Actually, they are worked in the same way as the place setting by simply following the charted design square by square, but they will take considerably longer to stitch and require more commitment to complete.

You may decide to build up a personal library of ethnic and exotic design sources to look through for inspiration when thinking about designing a new cross stitch project of your own. Magazine cuttings, colour brochures for exotic holidays and museum postcards provide a good basis for a collection covering these themes. You could hunt through shops selling second-hand art, ethnological and travel books and begin collecting a selection of these for future use. Always try to label and file your cuttings and postcards away neatly in cardboard files or boxes, so that they are easy to find when you need them, or you may decide to invest in a small filing cabinet to house your collection. Investigate all types of ethnic art including painting and sculpture, textiles (particularly woven and knitted patterns), pottery, costume and jewellery.

SCANDINAVIAN
RUNNER

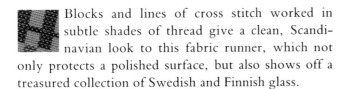 Blocks and lines of cross stitch worked in subtle shades of thread give a clean, Scandinavian look to this fabric runner, which not only protects a polished surface, but also shows off a treasured collection of Swedish and Finnish glass.

MATERIALS

- Pale grey 110 cm (43 in) wide 14 count Fine Aida evenweave fabric (Zweigart E3706, pewter 713)
- DMC stranded cotton in the following colours: purple 327; greys 413, 414, 415, 647
- Tapestry needle size 24
- Tacking thread in a dark colour
- Sewing needle and pins
- Embroidery hoop

MEASURING UP

Decide on the finished size of the runner, bearing in mind that this design will look best worked on a long, narrow rectangle of fabric. Add at least 10 cm (4 in) extra all round to allow you to mount the fabric comfortably in the embroidery hoop while stitching. Tack the finished size of the runner on the fabric.

PREPARING THE FABRIC

Along each short edge tack a guideline 8 cm (3 in) in from the finished edge. Work a line of tacking at right angles to the centre of the guideline. This line marks the centre of the first block of stitches to be worked.

WORKING THE EMBROIDERIES

1 Begin stitching at the centre of one short edge, noting that the guideline indicates the lower edge of the design. Mount the fabric in the embroidery hoop (page 19), and begin by working the block of nine stitches at the base of the design. Work in cross stitch (page 22) from the chart, using four strands of thread in the needle throughout and remembering that each square on the chart represents one cross stitch worked over two vertical and two horizontal woven blocks of fabric.
2 Work the remaining two blocks and short line of stitches to complete one repeat. Continue stitching repeats of the design towards the corner, making sure you leave a gap of approximately 4 cm (1½ in) of unworked fabric between the embroidery and the long

STITCHED IN grey and purple, the regular pattern of blocks contrasts well with the colours and shapes of modern glass. The design would be equally attractive worked on white fabric using bright primary colours, or you could choose light and dark shades of just one colour to coordinate with your curtains, cushions and wallpaper.

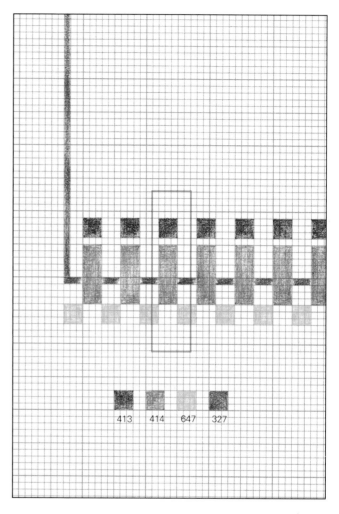

413 414 647 327

edge. You may need to make this gap larger or smaller to make sure that the last repeat fits on the runner.

3 Repeat this process in the opposite direction to complete one end of the runner. Check that all the blocks of stitches are complete and that the base of each lower block falls along the guideline.

4 Work the row of single cross stitches along one long edge, stopping 12 woven blocks short of the guideline across the short edge. Then work the same number of repeats along this edge and another single row of cross stitches along the remaining long edge.

MAKING UP THE RUNNER

1 Press the embroidery lightly on the wrong side with a warm iron. Cut the fabric to the required size, allowing a margin of 2.5 cm (1 in) for the hem allowance.

2 Pin and tack a narrow double hem (page 152) round the runner, turning in the corners neatly. Secure the hem with a row of back stitches worked over three or four woven blocks using three strands of grey 415.

JAPANESE
SCATTER CUSHIONS

 Based on Sashiko quilting, a type of traditional stitching worked in Japan, the strong geometric patterns are easy and to work providing you take care to count the stitches in each section accurately.

MATERIALS

- Dark blue 110 cm (43 in) wide 14 count Fine Aida evenweave fabric (Zweigart E3706, navy 589)
- DMC stranded cotton in cream 712
- Tapestry needle size 24
- Tacking thread in a light colour
- Matching sewing thread and zip fasteners
- Ready-made cushion pads
- Sewing needle and pins
- Large embroidery hoop or adjustable rectangular embroidery frame

MEASURING UP

Decide on the finished size of each cushion cover, bearing in mind that you will need sufficient fabric to make both the front and back. On the front, add at least 10 cm (4 in) extra all round to allow you to mount the fabric in your hoop or frame. The plain back of each cover is made in two pieces joined by a central seam with a zip fastener inserted, so you will need to add 5 cm (2 in) for the seam allowances, plus 2.5 cm (1 in) all round for turnings.

PREPARING THE FABRIC

Cut out the fabric for the front of each cushion and mark the finished size onto the fabric with lines of tacking, taking care that the lines of stitches run between two rows of woven blocks of fabric.

CUSHION A:

The design is worked in a central panel, leaving a wide margin of unworked fabric round the edge. Tack a vertical line through the centre of the fabric inside the tacked outline, taking care not to cross any vertical threads. Mark the central horizontal line in the same way. Mount the fabric in the embroidery hoop or frame (pages 19–20).

CUSHION B:

The embroidery is worked in a broad band across the cushion, so first mark out this band by tacking two lines 78 fabric blocks apart. Then find the centre of this

block by tacking a vertical line through the middle of the band, taking care not to cross any vertical threads. Then tack the central horizontal line in the same way. Mount the fabric in the embroidery hoop or frame.

CUSHION C:
This cushion features an all-over design. First tack a vertical line through the centre of the fabric, taking care not to cross any vertical threads. Mark the central horizontal line in the same way. Mount the fabric in the embroidery hoop or frame.

WORKING THE EMBROIDERY

CUSHION A:
Begin working in cross stitch (page 22) at the centre of the fabric and work four complete repeats of the design to form a square panel. Use four strands of thread and note that each pale square on the chart represents one stitch worked over two vertical and two horizontal woven blocks of fabric.

CUSHION B:
1 Begin working in cross stitch (page 22) at the centre of the marked band and work repeats of the design until the band is filled. Use four strands of thread and note that each pale square on the chart represents one stitch worked over two vertical and two horizontal woven blocks of fabric.
2 Work approximately 1.5 cm (½ in) extra at each end of the band to avoid an unsightly gap in the embroidery when the cover is stitched together.

CUSHION C:
1 Begin working in cross stitch (page 22) at the centre, repeating the design until the tacked area is filled. Use four strands of thread and note that each square on the chart represents one stitch worked over two vertical and two horizontal woven blocks of fabric.
2 Work approximately 1.5 cm (½ in) extra all round the cushion to avoid unsightly gaps.

MAKING UP THE CUSHION COVERS

Press the embroidery lightly on the wrong side. Cut out to the required size, allowing 2.5 cm (1 in) all round for the seam allowance. Follow the illustrated instructions on page 155 for making up the cushion covers.

SASHIKO designs also lend themselves to many other colour combinations including black with pale grey, brown with gold and deep pink with apple green.

ALTHOUGH THIS *design is intended to be worked in a central panel, it would be equally effective embroidered all over the front of the cushion cover in the same way as cushion C.*

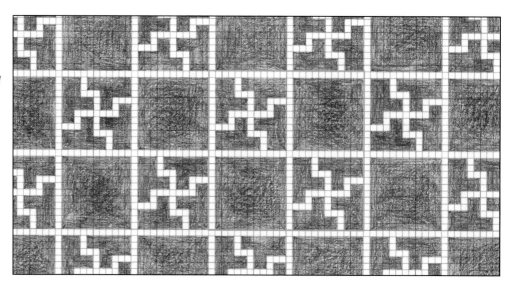

THIS DESIGN *would also look attractive stitched in bright colours of thread on white fabric. Try working the centre pattern in scarlet or emerald green, the outside stripes in royal blue and the single stitches in yellow.*

CHANGE THE *look of this design and work it in reverse by choosing a pastel shade for the background fabric and embroidering the lines with dark thread.*

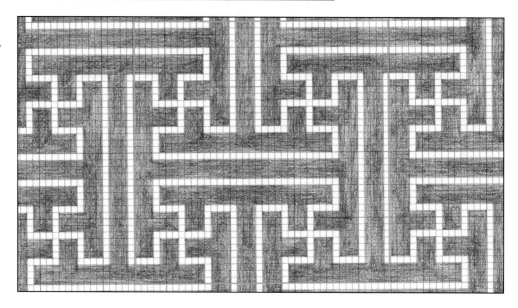

CHINESE BLUEBIRDS
OF HAPPINESS

Bluebirds denote happiness in Chinese mythology. In this picture, a pair of birds are set against a background decorated with the repeated symbol of longevity. The design is stitched mainly in shades of blue thread on white fabric, the traditional colours used for centuries in Chinese peasant cross stitch embroidery.

MATERIALS

- White 110 cm (43 in) wide 11 count Pearl Aida even-weave fabric (Zweigart E1007, colour 1)
- DMC stranded cotton in the following colours purple 333; blues 340, 791, 796, 798, 813
- Tapestry needle size 24
- Tacking thread in a dark colour
- Stitch and tear embroidery backing (optional)
- Sewing needle
- Adjustable rectangular embroidery frame or rectangular wooden stretcher
- Sturdy cardboard
- Strong linen carpet thread or very fine string

MEASURING UP

The embroidered area of the picture measures approximately 20 cm (8 in) square. To this you will need to add at least 10 cm (4 in) all round to allow for mounting the fabric in a frame in order to work the stitching, and to enable the finished embroidery to be laced round a piece of cardboard prior to framing. You may need to add a wider margin of fabric round the edge when working on a large embroidery frame or on a stretcher which cannot be adjusted.

PREPARING THE FABRIC

Cut out the fabric and tack a vertical line through the centre of the fabric, taking care not to cross any vertical threads. Mark the central horizontal line in the same way and mark the centre of the chart with a soft pencil. Mount the fabric in the embroidery frame or stretcher (page 20). If you are not an experienced stitcher, you may like to tack a piece of stitch and tear embroidery backing onto the wrong side of the fabric. This will give the fabric extra stability while you are stitching.

WORKING THE EMBROIDERY

1 Begin stitching at the centre of the design, noting that each coloured square on the chart represents one complete stitch worked over one woven block of fabric. Work the pair of bluebirds in cross stitch (page 22), using three strands of thread in the needle throughout.

2 When the birds have been completed, outline them and add the wing details in back stitch (page 22) using two strands of thread. Work each back stitch over one block of fabric.

3 Work the cloud outlines in back stitch using two strands of thread. Work carefully from the chart, stopping at intervals to check that the back stitch lines are in the correct position.

4 Finally, work the background pattern and border in cross stitch using three strands of thread.

FINISHING THE PICTURE

1 When all the embroidery has been completed, carefully tear away the embroidery backing close to the stitching, if used. Press the embroidery lightly on the wrong side over a well-padded surface. Use a warm iron and take care not to press down too hard and crush the stitching.

2 Decide on the size of frame and window mount for the picture, and then lace the embroidery (page 157) securely over a piece of sturdy card cut to the appropriate size. Use strong linen carpet thread or very fine string for the lacing.

3 Follow the suggestions given on page 157 for having your picture framed.

IDEAS TO INSPIRE

The idea of contrasting a pictorial image against a symmetrically patterned background would work well with some of the extra designs shown on the various pattern library pages. For example, the rabbit on page 115 surrounded by bright orange baby carrots arranged in a chequerboard pattern would make a lovely nursery picture, as would the tabby cat on the same page set off with rows of tiny mice.

Non-figurative backgrounds also work well: try experimenting with plaids, vertical, horizontal and diagonal stripes, and regular patterns of dots and dashes. Sketch out your ideas first on graph paper (see Experimenting, page 142), keeping the colours and arrangements fairly simple so as not to detract from the pictorial element of the design.

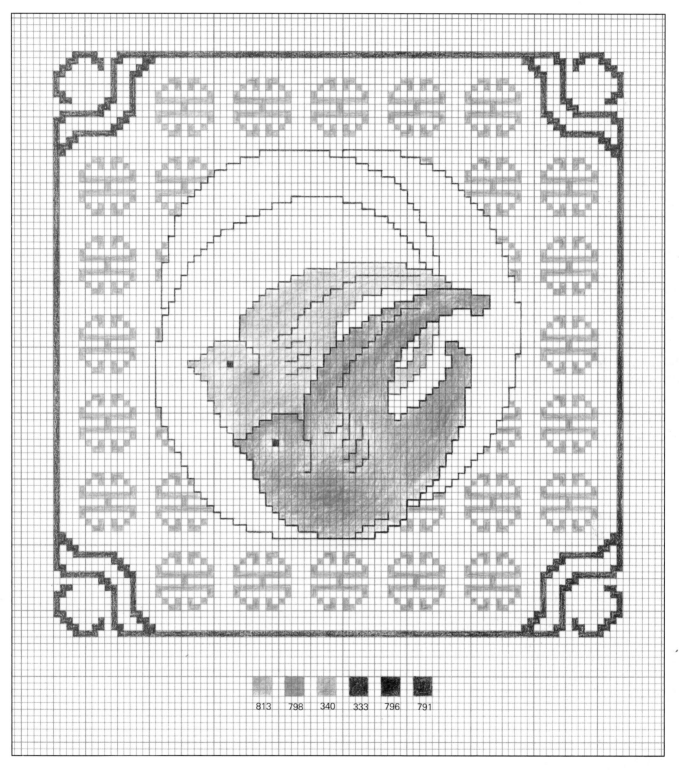

813	798	340	333	796	791

THE BLUEBIRD design could also be used to decorate a cushion or photograph album cover. It would work well stitched in tapestry wool on canvas, but you would then have to stitch the background colour as well.

THE BACK stitch outlines are indicated by blue lines on the chart. Work these after the birds have been completed.

EUROPEAN FOLK ART
PLACE SETTING

 These striking red and blue folk art motifs are quick and easy to stitch. Here, the two motifs decorate a tablemat and napkin, but experienced stitchers could use either of the designs to make a border round a tablecloth.

MATERIALS

- Cream 130 cm (51 in) wide 18 count Ainring even-weave fabric (Zweigart E3793, colour 264)
- DMC stranded cotton in the following colours: red 498; blue 797; cream 712
- Tapestry needle size 24
- Tacking thread in a dark colour
- Sewing needle and pins
- Small embroidery hoop

MEASURING UP

Traditionally, rectangular tablemats measure approximately 20 cm by 30 cm (8 in by 12 in), but they are often larger in the USA, approximately 30 cm by 45 cm (12 in by 18 in). To decide on the best size for your requirements, lay out a standard place setting of cutlery with two sizes of plate. You may like to include space on the tablemat for glasses and a side plate or, as here, place these items at the edge of the mat. Measure the area used and add 2.5 cm (1 in) all round for the hem allowance, plus a little extra to allow the fabric to be mounted easily in the hoop.

Napkins are usually square, varying in size from small tea napkins of 30 cm (12 in) to large dinner napkins of 60 cm (24 in). However, a good all-purpose size is 38 cm (15 in) square. Lengths of 130 cm (51 in) width fabric can be divided evenly for napkins of this size with sufficient left for hem allowances after trimming away the selvedges. From a 90 cm (36 in) length of fabric, you will be able to cut six napkins.

PREPARING THE FABRIC

TABLEMAT:
Tack two parallel guidelines to mark the position of the embroidery. Here, the band of motifs is placed about 2.5 cm (1 in) from the finished edge, and the band itself is worked over 38 woven blocks of fabric. You can extend the band right up to the finished edge on the two long sides, or position it centrally as shown.

NAPKIN:
Mark the position of the motif approximately 2.5 cm (1 in) from the finished edges on two adjacent sides.

WORKING THE EMBROIDERIES

Mount the fabric for the tablemat in the embroidery hoop (page 19), and begin stitching at the centre of the two tacked lines. Work in cross stitch (page 22) from the chart, using three strands of thread in the needle throughout. Each square on the chart represents one cross stitch worked over two vertical and two horizon-

498   797

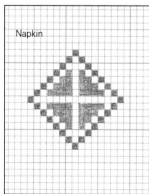

Napkin

tal woven blocks of fabric. Work the napkin motif in the same way as the tablemat motif.

MAKING UP THE PLACE SETTING

1 Press the embroidery lightly on the wrong side. Cut away any surplus fabric round the tablemat, allowing a margin of 2.5 cm (1 in) for the hem allowance.

2 Pin and tack a narrow double hem (page 152) round the edge. Secure with back stitches (page 22) worked close to the turned-over edge. Work each stitch over two or three blocks using three strands of cream 712.

STRONGLY contrasting thread colours add interest to a plain soup plate. You can achieve a different effect by choosing a more subtle colour combination to harmonize with your own crockery, perhaps using a light and dark tone of the same colour.

AFRICAN
BAG

Decorate the front of a fabric bag with a geometric border pattern inspired by an African mural. The design is stitched in shades of orange, tan and rust on fabric with a natural, unbleached finish.

MATERIALS

- Natural 130 cm (51 in) wide 14 count Rustico evenweave fabric (Zweigart E3953, colour 54)
- Matching cotton fabric for lining
- DMC stranded cotton in the following colours: orange 741, 608; tan 922; rust 919
- Tapestry needle size 24
- Tacking thread in a dark colour
- Sewing needle and pins
- Matching sewing thread
- Embroidery hoop or adjustable rectangular frame

MEASURING UP

The finished bag measures 42 cm (16½ in) deep and 36 cm (14 in) wide. You will need one piece of fabric for the front and one for the back. Add a margin approximately 10 cm (4 in) all round the finished size for the front. For the back, add 2.5 cm (1 in) to the width and 6 cm (2¼ in) to the depth. Cut two pieces of lining to the same size as the finished back, plus 1.5 cm (½ in) all round for turnings. You will also need two pieces of fabric 40 cm by 8 cm (16 in by 3 in) to make the handles.

PREPARING THE FABRIC

On the front, mark the finished size of the bag with a row of tacking. Tack a guideline 5 cm (2 in) down from the top of the bag. This line marks the top of the embroidered band. Work another row of tacking at right angles to the guideline to mark the centre of the band.

WORKING THE EMBROIDERY

1 Draw a line down the centre of the chart with a soft pencil. Mount the fabric in the hoop (page 19).
2 Work the design in cross stitch (page 22) from the chart, using three strands of thread in the needle throughout. Begin at the centre of the band and work outwards, remembering that each square on the chart represents one cross stitch worked over two vertical and two horizontal fabric blocks.

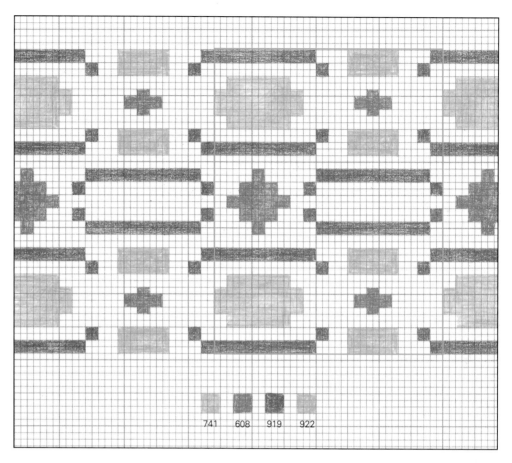

741   608   919   922

MAKE THIS useful bag and carry your groceries home from a shopping expedition in style. You could easily make one in a larger size and substitute waterproof fabric for the cotton lining, so that the bag can be used to transport a damp swimming costume and towel or a sports kit.

MAKING UP THE BAG

1 Press the embroidery lightly on the wrong side with a warm iron. Cut away the surplus fabric on the front, leaving the same allowance for turnings as on the back.

2 Pin and tack the back and front together with right sides facing, and stitch round the sides and base, taking a seam allowance of 1.5 cm (½ in). Clip the lower corners (page 155). Repeat with the lining pieces.

3 Turn over 4.5 cm (1¾ in) round the bag top, then pin and tack in place. Turn over 1.5 cm (½ in) round the lining top, then pin and tack in place.

4 Fold the handle strips in half lengthways and turn in the raw edges. Pin, tack and machine stitch all round to make two handles. On the inside of the bag, pin and tack one handle to the front and one to the back, overlapping the tacked hem with the ends of the handles.

5 Turn the bag right side out. Work three spaced rows of machine stitching round the top of the bag to secure the handles. Slide the lining into the bag, wrong sides together. Matching the bag and lining seams, pin the lining to the top of the bag, taking care not to catch in the handles. Slipstitch the lining (page 152) in place.

Folk Art Borders

Folk Art Borders

Folk Art Motifs

Japanese Sashiko Designs

Patterns from African Murals

American Indian Designs

CHAPTER FIVE

HEARTH
& HOME
DESIGNS

INTRODUCTION

....

Today, hand embroidery is very much a domestic pleasure and an enjoyable way of spending part of your leisure time creating something which is uniquely personal. In this chapter and the pattern libraries, you will find everything you need to create your own piece of cross stitch embroidery. Keep your work to ensure that it becomes a twentieth-century heirloom, or present it to a family member or friend as a delightful and unique gift.

Christmas cards and tree decorations make the perfect introduction to cross stitch embroidery. Bold and colourful, the festive designs on page 84 are quick and simple to stitch and have the added advantage of being sufficiently small to work in the hand without an embroidery hoop. There are five designs for card motifs and three for tree decorations, plus a further selection in the pattern library on page 165. Ready-made presentation cards simplify the finishing-off stage, although you could cut your own mounts from thin cardboard if you prefer. You may also like to add 'Merry Xmas' or another seasonal greeting to your card using the tiny back stitch alphabet on page 160. The circular golden frames used for the tree decorations are available in several other shapes and sizes, all with a simple, push-in back panel to secure the embroidery. Hang the decorations from your tree with loops of red or green satin ribbon.

Stitch a border of repeated holly leaf motifs round the edge of a tablecloth to make a really special setting for a delicious Christmas lunch. Make personalized Christmas gifts for under the tree by using the seasonal designs to decorate some of the other small projects, for example, the pincushions on page 123 and the paperweight and porcelain box on page 37. Fold the finished gifts in white tissue paper and place in a suitable box before giftwrapping. You can make your own special wrapping paper by decorating large sheets of ordinary graph paper with brightly coloured cross stitch designs filled in with coloured pencils and felt pens. Make matching gift tags by sticking a small square of the decorated paper onto thin card, punching a hole close to one corner to hold a length of metallic gold ribbon.

The pot-pourri sachets on page 89 are also simple to stitch and make a thoughtful gift. They are filled with a mixture of pot-pourri and polyster stuffing, but you could substitute dried lavender or rose petals for the pot-pourri. The same technique can be used to fill a herb pillow, adding hops and sweetly-scented dried herbs to the stuffing to ensure a good night's rest.

The house and garden sampler on page 74 is one of the most complex projects in the book but the finished result will repay the many hours you spend stitching the design. Make a habit of checking each small section regularly for mistakes while you are working since tiny errors of just one stitch more or less in the border, for example, may be impossible to correct once the design has been finished. The sampler can be worked according to the chart on page 76, or you may wish to substitute your own inscription for the alphabet shown beneath the cottage. Draw out your chosen wording on graph paper, taking care with the spacing of the individual letters. You will need to alter the dimensions of the border round the edge of the sampler to accommodate your inscription if it takes up more space than the alphabet on the chart. The chapter on experimenting (page 140) gives details of how to do this successfully. To design your own sampler, select several appropriate motifs plus a border and alphabet from the various pattern library pages, then arrange them on graph paper to make a working chart (page 142). A sketch or photograph of your own house or flat can be adapted into a cross stitch chart (page 142) and used instead of the thatched cottage in the picture.

An embroidered picture makes a delightful gift for many occasions. The cupid picture on page 87 would be lovely stitched as an engagement or wedding present, or for a special anniversary. Included in the pattern libraries are pictorial zodiac signs (pages 94–95) as well as zodiac symbols (page 164). A pictorial birth sign would make a lovely centrepiece for a gift sampler celebrating the birth of a child, or a nursery picture for a toddler. Add a simple geometric border (page 134) around the edge, or repeat the appropriate zodiac symbol at each corner, then mount the embroidery in a simple, brightly-coloured picture frame.

Initials and monograms can be used in a variety of ways to personalize garments and household linen. The corner of the napkin on page 82 is decorated with a traditional letterform surrounded by tiny flower motifs. For a more modern effect, choose the appropriate initial from the alphabet on page 90 and add a small geometric motif instead of flowers. Work initials and monograms on fabric without an even weave by using the waste canvas method described on page 21.

Monograms incorporate two or more letters, overlapped or intertwined to make a decorative device, and they have similar uses to initials. The alphabets on pages 90 and 91 will provide you with a good starting point for your design. The simplest monograms consist of two letters such as 'H' and 'D' placed next to each other with their vertical strokes aligned. You could add a line of single cross stitches to frame the monogram, or one of the flower sprigs on page 42. Alternatively, trace off a single letter from your chosen alphabet, then trace a second one over the top, letting it overlap or interlock with the first. When stitching a monogram on a sheet or handkerchief where both sides of the fabric may show, you can use one of the double-sided variations of ordinary cross stitch (page 23) which form neat crosses or lines on the reverse.

Letterforms can be grouped to create an unusual graphic image, laid out simply from A to Z or by using the letters to spell out an appropriate motto or short saying. When selecting the alphabet for your motto sampler, spend some time over your choice, since the style of lettering will be more appropriate when it reflects the sentiment of the words. For example, a sweet, old-fashioned motto like 'A Thing of Beauty is a Joy Forever' or 'Home Sweet Home' would look much more effective stitched in traditional letterforms than would a verse from a contemporary song or poem. Choice of colour is also important, both for the fabric and threads, and it is a good idea to work small samples of your chosen colour scheme before starting to stitch.

The alphabet sampler illustrated on page 79 makes good use of the contrast between different sizes and styles of lettering. The letters create a bold pattern across the fabric without needing any additional decorative elements, and this design is enhanced by the use of strong colours. The alphabet on page 162 would look effective arranged in a similar way and, to add interest, the geometric pattern on the letters can be embroidered with several contrasting colours of thread.

HOUSE & GARDEN
SAMPLER

Houses have been a popular theme for samplers and embroidered pictures for centuries. This pretty, colour-washed cottage roofed with thatch is typically English, nestling in its lush garden of colourful plants and shrubs.

MATERIALS

- White 110 cm (43 in) wide 11 count Pearl Aida even-weave fabric (Zweigart E1007, colour 1)
- DMC stranded cotton in the following colours: pinks 335, 604, 818; purples 208, 333; orange 740; yellow 726; turquoise 993; blues 794, 796, 798, 809; greens 470, 907, 910, 912, 943, 958, 989, 3348; grey 413; browns 420, 435, 840, 3772
- Tapestry needle size 24
- Tacking thread in a dark colour
- Stitch and tear embroidery backing (optional)
- Sewing needle
- Adjustable rectangular embroidery frame or rectangular wooden stretcher
- Sturdy cardboard
- Strong linen carpet thread or very fine string

MEASURING UP

The embroidery measures approximately 29 cm by 38 cm (11½ in by 15 in). To this you will need to add at least 10 cm (4 in) all round to allow for mounting the fabric in a frame in order to work the stitching, and to enable the finished embroidery to be laced round a piece of cardboard prior to framing. You may need to add a wider margin of fabric round the edge when working on a large embroidery frame or on a stretcher which cannot be adjusted.

PREPARING THE FABRIC

Cut out the rectangle of fabric and tack a vertical line through the centre, taking care not to cross any vertical threads. Mark the central horizontal line in the same way and mark the centre of the chart with a soft pencil. Mount the fabric in the frame or stretcher (page 20). If

DESIGNED FOR the more experienced stitcher, this complex sampler design will prove quite a challenge to work.

818 840 3772 435 794 413 726 208

910 809 798 796

335

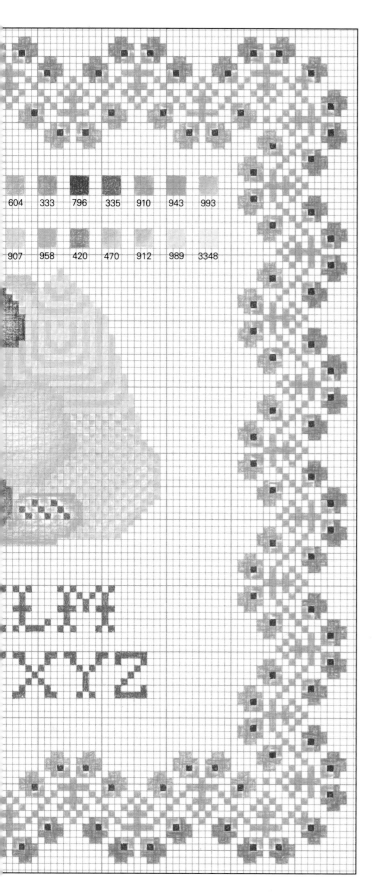

604	333	796	335	910	943	993
907	958	420	470	912	989	3348

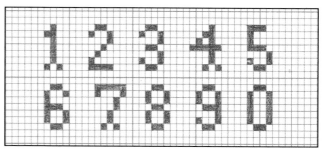

YOU MAY prefer to substitute a name and date for the alphabet worked below the cottage.

Sketch out the arrangement of letters and numbers on graph paper (page 143) before starting.

you are not very experienced at embroidery, tack a piece of stitch and tear embroidery backing onto the wrong side of the fabric. This will give the fabric stability during the stitching.

WORKING THE EMBROIDERY

1 Begin stitching at the centre of the design, noting that each coloured square shown on the chart represents one stitch worked over one woven block of fabric. Much of the design is worked in cross stitch (page 22), with the cottage walls and door worked in half cross stitch (page 22). The thatched roof is also worked in half cross stitch, but here the stitches on every row face in alternate directions to give a zig-zag effect. Using three strands of thread, work carefully from the chart, stopping at intervals to check that all the stitches are in the correct position.

2 When the cottage, plants and shrubs have been completed, outline the thatched roof in back stitch (page 22) using two strands of thread. Work each back stitch over one block of fabric.

3 Work rows of back stitch diagonally across the window panes using a single strand of grey thread. Outline the letter box and door knob with back stitch and one strand of thread. Work the alphabet and the border in cross stitch using three strands of thread.

FINISHING THE PICTURE

1 When all the embroidery has been completed, carefully tear away the embroidery backing close to the stitching, if used. Press the embroidery lightly on the wrong side with a warm iron.

2 Decide on the size of frame for the picture, and then lace the embroidery (page 157) securely over a piece of sturdy card cut to the appropriate size. Use strong linen carpet thread or very fine string for the lacing.

ALPHABET
SAMPLER

 Alphabets have been an important feature of samplers since the time they progressed from being merely a way of sampling various stitches and designs before working a piece of embroidery. Here, five different alphabets are combined to create a striking graphic image which is stitched in a variety of strong colours. Other alphabets are illustrated in the pattern library sections, and you may like to experiment with these and design your own alphabet sampler, perhaps adding a narrow, geometric border to frame the letters.

MATERIALS

- White 110 cm (43 in) wide 11 count Pearl Aida even-weave fabric (Zweigart E1007, colour 1)
- DMC stranded cotton in the following colours: pink 3607; red 816; orange 971; yellow 973; kingfisher blue 996; blue 796; green 906
- Tapestry needle size 24
- Tacking thread in a dark colour
- Stitch and tear embroidery backing (optional)
- Sewing needle
- Adjustable rectangular embroidery frame or rectangular wooden stretcher
- Sturdy cardboard
- Strong linen carpet thread or very fine string

MEASURING UP

The embroidered area of the picture measures approximately 18 cm × 25 cm (7 in × 10 in). To this you will need to add at least 10 cm (4 in) all round to allow for mounting the fabric in a frame in order to work the stitching, and to enable the finished embroidery to be laced round a piece of cardboard prior to framing. You may need to add a wider margin of fabric round the edge when working on a large embroidery frame or on a stretcher which cannot be adjusted.

PREPARING THE FABRIC

Cut out the fabric and tack a vertical line through the centre of the fabric, taking care not to cross any vertical threads. Mark the central horizontal line in the same way and mark the centre of the chart with a soft pencil. Mount the fabric in the embroidery frame or stretcher (page 20). If you are not an experienced stitcher, you may like to tack a piece of stitch and tear embroidery backing onto the wrong side of the fabric. This will give the fabric extra stability while you are stitching, and help to prevent puckering.

WORKING THE EMBROIDERY

1 Begin stitching at the centre of the design, noting that each coloured square shown on the chart represents one complete stitch worked over one woven block of fabric. Work the letters in cross stitch (page 22), using three strands of thread in the needle throughout.
2 Work carefully from the chart, stopping at intervals to check that the individual letters are spaced correctly and that the top diagonal of each cross faces in the same direction.

FINISHING THE PICTURE

1 When all the embroidery has been completed, carefully tear away the embroidery backing close to the stitching, if used. Press the embroidery lightly on the wrong side over a well-padded surface. Use a warm iron and take care not to press down too hard and crush the stitching.
2 Decide on the size of frame and window mount for the picture, and then lace the embroidery (page 157) securely over a piece of sturdy card cut to the appropriate size. Use strong linen carpet thread or very fine string for the lacing.
3 Follow the suggestions given on page 157 for having your picture framed.

IDEAS TO INSPIRE

An alphabet sampler makes a good project for a fairly inexperienced stitcher to tackle. Each letter is completed before going on to the next and the changes of colour, scale and style between the rows prevent the stitching from becoming repetitive. The first three letters can be worked alone to make a tiny gift sampler to greet the arrival of a new baby. Work the letters in shades of pink or blue, perhaps adding a tiny flower or another appropriate motif from one of the pattern library pages.

THE LETTERS are stitched here in a range of bold, contrasting colours but the design would look quite different but equally striking worked in a single distinctive colour.

STITCH EACH *letter carefully from the chart, making sure that each one is spaced correctly and that the base of each row shares the same line of holes across the fabric.*

973   3607   796   906   996   816   971

INITIALLED
NAPKINS

 Stitch a set of spotless white napkins and trim each of them with a decorated initial. Napkins are quick and simple to embroider, and a set bearing the appropriate initials would make a delightful present for family and friends alike.

MATERIALS

- White 130 cm (51 in) wide 18 count Damask Aida evenweave fabric (Zweigart E3239, colour 1)
- DMC stranded cotton in the following colours: pink 603; purple 552; kingfisher blue 995; greens 699, 906
- Tapestry needle size 24
- Tacking thread in a dark colour
- Matching sewing thread
- Sewing needle and pins
- Small embroidery hoop

MEASURING UP

Napkins are usually square, varying in size from small tea napkins of 30 cm (12 in) to large dinner napkins of 60 cm (24 in). Decide on a size which will suit you, adding 2 cm (¾ in) all round for the hem allowance. However, when using this type of evenweave fabric, a good all-purpose size for a napkin is 38 cm (15 in) square. Lengths of 130 cm (51 in) wide fabric can be divided evenly for napkins of this size with sufficient left for hem allowances after trimming away the selvedges. From a 90 cm (36 in) length of fabric, you will be able to cut a set of six napkins.

PREPARING THE FABRIC

Cut the fabric into pieces of the required size and mark the position of each initial with vertical and horizontal lines of tacking. Keep the initial approximately 6 cm (2¼ in) from the finished edges on two adjacent sides of the napkin.

WORKING THE EMBROIDERY

Begin stitching at the edge of the tacked rectangle. Mount the corner of the fabric in the embroidery hoop

EACH COLOURED square represents one stitch worked over two vertical and two horizontal woven blocks of fabric.

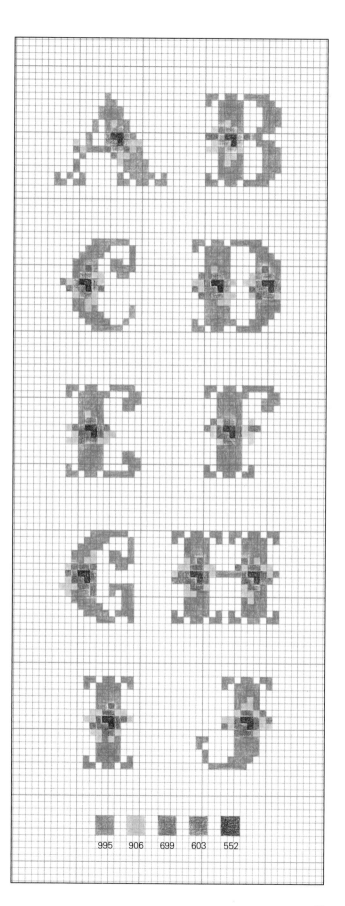

| 995 | 906 | 699 | 603 | 552 |

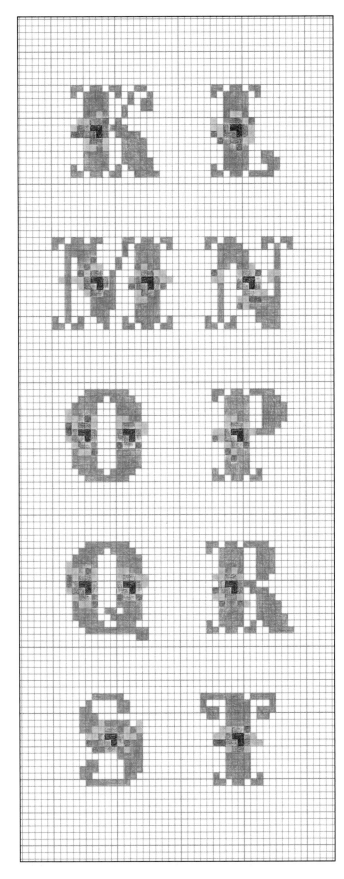

MAKE A set of initialled napkins, choosing thread colours to coordinate with your tableware. You may prefer to work a simpler initial for everyday napkins. Choose one from the selection shown on the pattern library pages (90–91).

THE CHART shown at the bottom right-hand corner of the opposite page shows the letter 'A' decorated with two tiny flower and leaf motifs. Use these motifs to decorate the other letters of the alphabet.

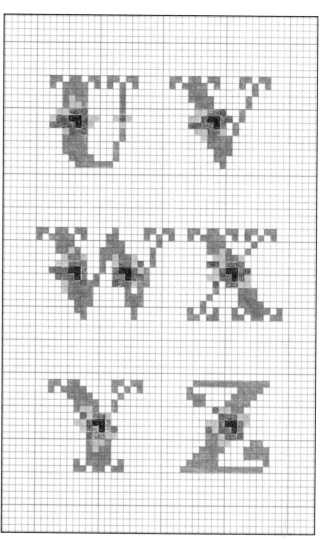

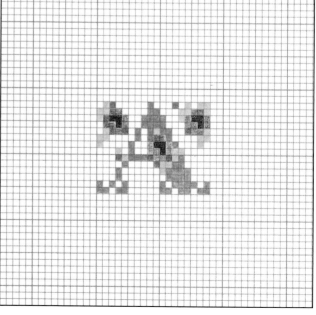

(page 19) and work in cross stitch (page 22) from the chart, using three strands of thread in the needle throughout. Each square on the chart represents one cross stitch worked over two vertical and two horizontal woven blocks of fabric.

MAKING UP THE NAPKIN

1 Press the embroidery carefully on the wrong side with a warm iron, pressing down lightly and taking care not to crush the stitches.

2 Pin and tack a narrow double hem (page 152) round the edge, turning in the corners neatly. Secure the hem with hemming stitch worked by hand (page 152), or a row of machine stitching.

CHRISTMAS CARDS
AND TREE DECORATIONS

....

Make your own colourful greetings cards and tree decorations to celebrate the joys of Christmas. Quick to stitch, the designs are all small enough to be worked in the hand.

MATERIALS

....

CHRISTMAS CARDS:
- Scraps of white 18 count Damask Aida evenweave fabric (Zweigart E3239, colour 1)
- DMC stranded cotton in these colours: reds 606, 666; orange 971; yellow 973; kingfisher blue 995; greens 699, 703; greys 318, 413; rust 920; brown 3021
- DMC presentation cards

TREE DECORATIONS:
- Scraps of white 18 count Damask Aida evenweave fabric (Zweigart E3239, colour 1)
- DMC stranded cotton in the following colours: red 666; greens 699, 703
- Circular DMC decorative frames N870
- Narrow scarlet satin ribbon

WORKING THE EMBROIDERIES

....

1 Fold the fabric pieces in four and mark each centre with a pin, then mark the centre of each chart.

2 Work the design outwards from the centre in cross stitch (page 22) from the charts using three strands of thread in a size 24 tapestry needle.

3 Add veins to the holly leaves in back stitch (page 22), following the lines on the charts. Add outlines and details to the card designs in the same way. Work French knots (page 23) in red 666 to make holly berries.

MAKING UP THE CARDS
AND TREE DECORATIONS

....

1 Press lightly on the wrong side with a warm iron.

2 To finish the Christmas cards, measure the cutout window in the card, then cut away the surplus fabric from round the edge of the embroidery, allowing a margin of 1.5 cm (½ in) all round. Position the embroidery behind the window, turn the card face down and secure on the wrong side with adhesive tape. Stick the inside flap down over the embroidery with glue or double-sided adhesive tape.

3 Mount the holly embroideries in the gold frames, then add a ribbon loop to each decoration.

ALL THE *Christmas designs are worked on the same scale and each coloured square on the chart represents one cross stitch worked over two vertical and two horizontal woven blocks of fabric. Each back stitch is worked over two fabric blocks, and three strands of thread are used throughout.*

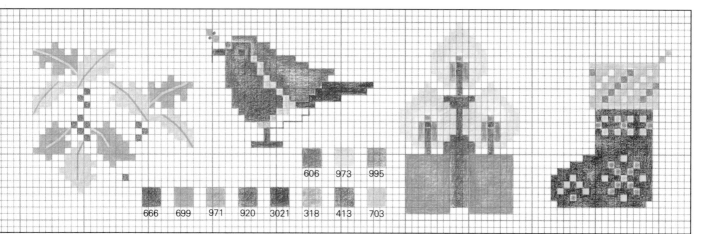

					606	973	995
666	699	971	920	3021	318	413	703

85

GOD
OF LOVE

 Cupid, the Roman god of love, is an apt subject for a picture specially embroidered to celebrate a happy event.

MATERIALS

- White 110 cm (43 in) wide 11 count Pearl Aida even-weave fabric (Zweigart E1007, colour 1)
- DMC stranded cotton in the following colours: flesh pink 3770; pinks 602, 957; yellows 725, 972; turquoise 993; blue 3755; green 704; beige 677; light tan 922
- Tapestry needle size 24
- Tacking thread in a dark colour
- Stitch and tear embroidery backing (optional)
- Sewing needle
- Adjustable rectangular embroidery frame
- Sturdy cardboard
- Strong linen carpet thread or very fine string

MEASURING UP

The embroidered portion of the picture covers an area approximately 15 cm (6 in) square. To this you will need to add at least 10 cm (4 in) all round to allow for mounting the fabric in a frame in order to work the stitching, and to enable the finished embroidery to be laced round a piece of cardboard prior to framing. You may need to add a wider margin of fabric round the edge when working on a large embroidery frame or on a stretcher which cannot be adjusted.

PREPARING THE FABRIC

Cut out the fabric and tack a vertical line through the centre of the fabric, taking care not to cross any vertical threads. Mark the central horizontal line in the same way and mark the centre of the chart with a soft pencil. Mount the fabric in the embroidery frame or stretcher (page 20). If you are not an experienced stitcher, you may like to tack a piece of stitch and tear embroidery backing onto the wrong side of the fabric. This will give the fabric extra stability while you are stitching.

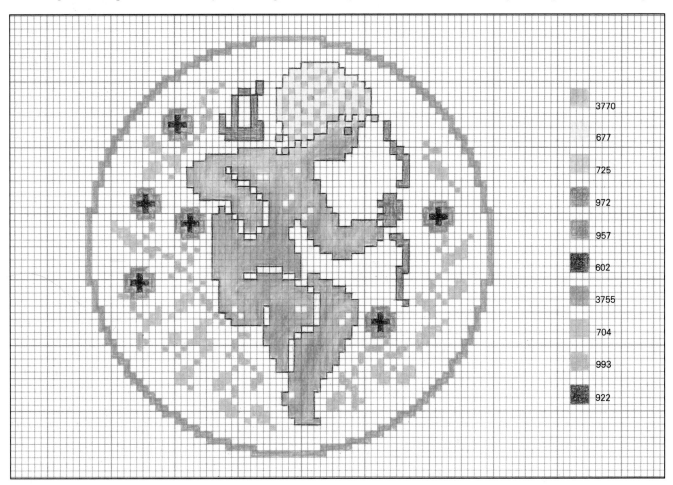

3770
677
725
972
957
602
3755
704
993
922

THE BACK stitch outlines are indicated on the chart. Work these after the cupid, quiver and bow have been completed in cross stitch.

THE PROPORTIONS of the cupid design have been enhanced by a perfectly-cut card mount and narrow wooden frame.

WORKING THE EMBROIDERY

1 Begin stitching at the centre of the design, noting that each coloured square shown on the chart represents one complete stitch worked over one woven block of fabric. Work the cupid, bow and quiver in cross stitch (page 22) using three strands of thread in the needle throughout.

2 When these elements have been completed, outline them in back stitch (page 22) using two strands of thread. Work each back stitch over one block of fabric.

3 Work the flower sprigs and circular border in cross stitch using three strands of thread. Work carefully from the chart, stopping at intervals to check that the flowers, leaves and stems are in their correct positions.

FINISHING THE PICTURE

1 When all the embroidery has been completed, carefully tear away the embroidery backing close to the stitching, if used. Press the embroidery lightly on the wrong side over a well-padded surface. Use a warm iron and take care not to press down too hard and crush the stitching.

2 Decide on the size of frame and window mount for the picture, and then lace the embroidery (page 157) securely over a piece of sturdy card cut to the appropriate size. Use strong linen carpet thread or very fine string for the lacing.

3 Follow the suggestions given on page 157 for having your picture framed.

LACY
POT-POURRI SACHETS

 Make one of these delightful heart-embroidered sachets and fill it with fragrant pot-pourri. Put one in a chest of drawers to scent your lingerie or add a ribbon tag and hang it in your wardrobe.

MATERIALS

- Small piece of blue 110 cm (43 in) wide 14 count Fine Aida evenweave fabric (Zweigart E3706, colour colonial blue 522)
- DMC stranded cotton in the following colours: white; pinks 603, 917; red 606
- Tapestry needle size 24
- Tacking thread in a light colour
- Matching sewing thread
- Sewing needle and pins
- Knitting needle
- Pot-pourri
- Polyester toy stuffing
- Embroidery hoop

MEASURING UP

You will need one piece of fabric for the front and one for the back of each sachet you make. The finished sizes of the sachets are as follows: single heart – 10.5 cm (4¼ in) square, four hearts – 12 cm (4¾ in) square. You will need to add 1.5 cm (½ in) all round to both front and back pieces for the seam allowance, plus a margin to allow you to mount the fabric in the hoop.

PREPARING THE FABRIC

First tack a vertical line through the centre of the fabric, taking care not to cross any vertical threads. Mark the central horizontal line in the same way and mark the centre of the chart with a soft pencil. Mount the fabric in the embroidery hoop (page 19).

WORKING THE EMBROIDERY

1 Begin working the heart shapes in cross stitch (page 22) using three strands of thread throughout and noting that each square on the chart represents one stitch worked over two vertical and two horizontal woven blocks of fabric.

2 Next, stitch the lace and ribbon border. To work the waved edging, make a half cross stitch (page 22) to fill each triangular shape shown on the chart.

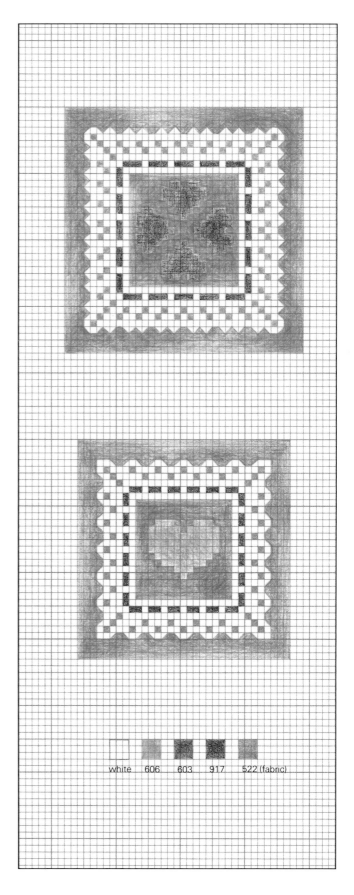

white   606   603   917   522 (fabric)

THE LACE effect is created by working white cross stitches over a blue background and leaving small blocks unstitched. Work half cross stitches wherever a triangular shape appears on the charts, to give an attractive waved edge to the outside of the design.

WHEN FILLING the sachets, choose strongly scented pot-pourri which contains quite large pieces and mix it with polyester stuffing, so that the surface of the filled sachets is smooth and firm. To make a hanging sachet, stitch a loop of matching satin ribbon to one corner of the sachet.

MAKING UP THE SACHETS

1 Press the embroidery lightly on the wrong side with a warm iron. Cut the front to the required size, allowing 1.5 cm (½ in) all round for the seam allowance.

2 Place the front and back pieces together with right sides facing. Pin and tack together, then machine stitch twice round the edge with matching thread just outside the last row of embroidery. Leave an unstitched section along one side.

3 Clip the corners (page 155) and turn the sachet right side out, taking care to push out each corner gently with the point of the knitting needle.

4 Stuff the sachet firmly with a mixture of pot-pourri and polyester toy stuffing, using the point of the knitting needle to help manoeuvre stuffing into each corner.

5 Slipstitch (page 152) the opening closed using matching thread.

Alphabets for Monograms

Alphabets for Monograms

Sampler Borders

Sampler Borders

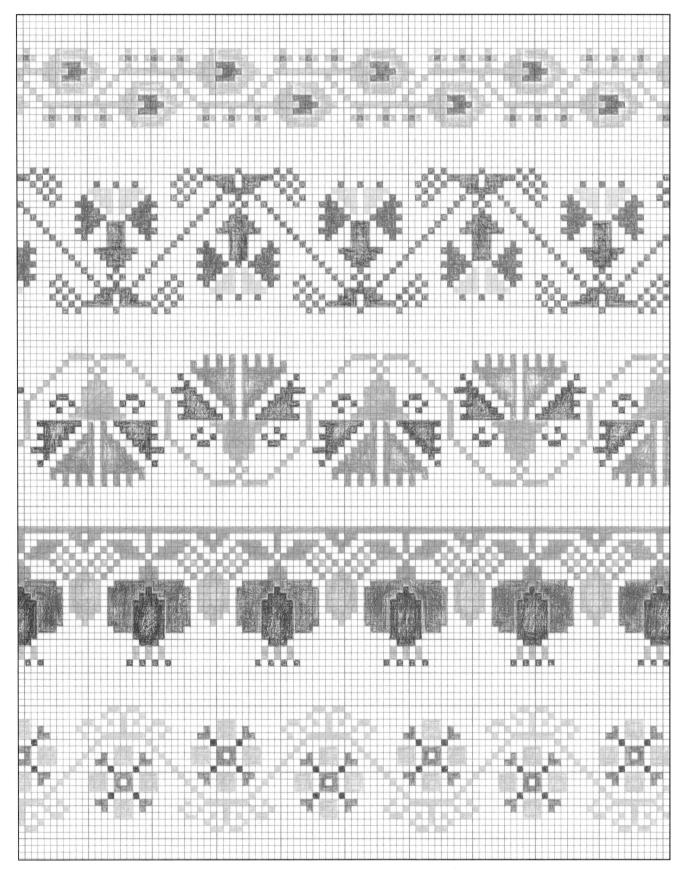

Small Alphabets for Greetings Cards

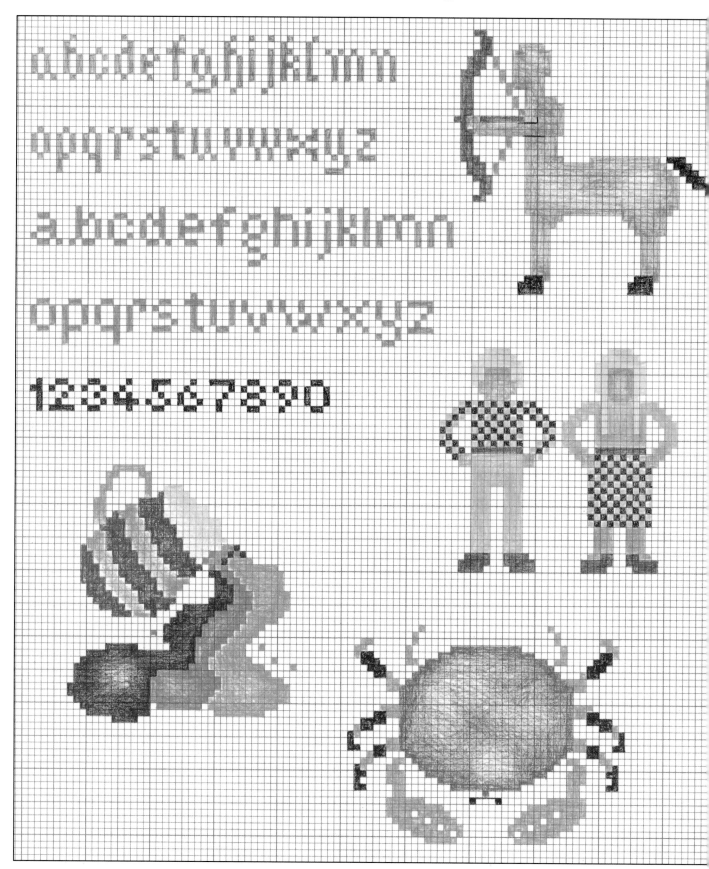

Zodiac Motifs

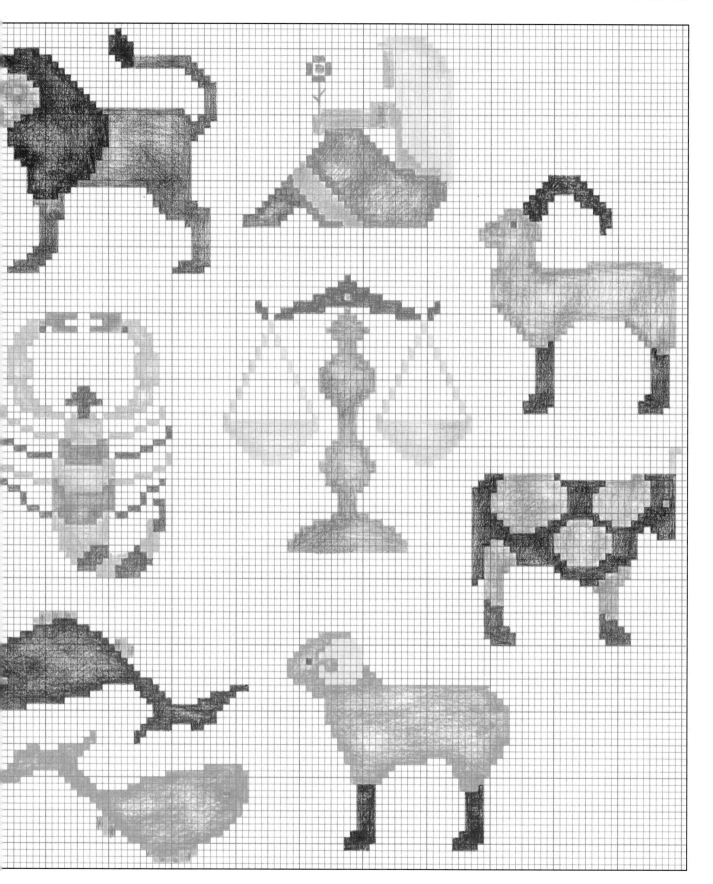

CHAPTER SIX

NATURAL
DESIGNS

INTRODUCTION

. . . .

The word 'natural' conjures up a multitude of images, many of which are so familiar that we are rather inclined to take them for granted. The beauties of the natural world offer unlimited scope for all kinds of cross stitch embroidery designs. Trees, forests and landscapes; fruits and berries; the rainbow; birds, animals, butterflies and insects; seascapes, sea creatures and shells; rocks and minerals – the list of natural wonders to inspire you is almost endless.

Today, due to an ever-increasing concern about ecology and global conservation, we are being made more aware of our surroundings and of man's effect on the planet. We can all take an active interest in expressing this concern, even in a modest way, by recycling waste materials, using environmentally-friendly products instead of chemicals, and turning a corner of our garden into a natural wilderness in order to provide a haven for local wildlife. The project and pattern library designs in this chapter reflect this newly-awakened delight in nature.

The design on the crunchy carrot apron (page 100) is not only bold and eye-catching, but also relatively quick to stitch. The orange carrot shapes are worked in half cross stitch outlined with back stitch, leaving just the leaves embroidered in cross stitch. You may prefer to work just one or two carrot motifs on a separate piece of contrasting fabric, bind it with matching binding and apply it to the body of the apron to make a pocket. Several of the larger designs in the pattern library at the end of the chapter would look good on an apron, particularly the tabby cat on page 115 and the two tropical fish with the wave pattern on page 117.

The swan design on page 103 and its companion, the goose design on page 116, can be used to decorate a pair of cushion covers, or you may prefer to stitch them as pictures. They are both straightforward to work, providing you begin at the centre of the design and work outwards, taking care to work the stitches accurately from the charts. Both the swan and the goose are designed to be embroidered onto a pale blue background, but you could substitute another colour and then embroider the sky area with shaded pale blue thread. Included in the pattern library are two more designs which can be used in a similar way. Work repeats of the topiary arch design (page 114) to fill a wide, shallow rectangular shape, using a mixture of both shaded and solid coloured threads. The quartet of gloriously coloured, exotic butterflies alighting on a leafy branch (page 117) will fit an upright rectangle and you could alter the thread colours so that the finished embroidery coordinates with its intended setting.

Both the butterfly borders on page 106 and the cherries on page 105 are fairly easy to stitch. Remember to start stitching at the centre of the strip so that the design is symmetrical at each end of the strip. The cherry shelf-edging is finished off along the lower edge with narrow lace edging. You can either buy the lace edging or crochet your own following one of the patterns given on page 148. Make sure you use a pre-shrunk thread to avoid the lace edging tightening up when the strips are washed.

The pattern library at the end of this chapter illustrates ten more border designs which you could use instead of the butterfly borders or the cherries. There are various other ways to use these border patterns: repeated round the edge of a tablecloth or across the ends of a long runner, along the top of a sheet or duvet cover using the waste canvas technique shown on page 21, or worked round the hem of a child's dress or pinafore. You can also separate out single motifs such as the bumble bee and use these separately in the same way as the shells on the mat on page 108. Work a group of strawberries and leaves at each corner of a crisp white tablecloth to make the perfect setting for a hot summer day's picnic.

A nursery picture should be bright and colourful enough to attract and keep your child's attention. The swimming fish on page 111 are great fun and could provide the basis for many a 'fishy' bedtime story. For children who are just getting to grips with letters, stitch the picture and include some appropriate wording beneath the image to help them polish their reading skills. Perhaps 'F is for Fish' or 'Two striped fish swimming in a fish bowl'. You can use the same approach with a picture based on other designs in this chapter, particularly the brightly-coloured toucan on page 116 and the cat family on page 115.

When working a large cross stitch design for a cushion cover or picture, use a large embroidery hoop or rectangular frame to hold your fabric. Fabric can be evenly stretched in a hoop or frame and you will then be able to work the embroidery stitches neatly and accurately without the fabric weave becoming distorted and pulling out of shape. Stitch and tear embroidery backing is useful when working on a large, solidly-stitched design. This is a non-woven fabric, rather like soft interlining, which is tacked onto the back of the fabric to give stability to the weave while you are stitching. The stitches are worked through both the embroidery fabric and the backing. After the design has been completed, the backing is carefully torn away round the stitched areas.

Many experienced stitchers like to create their own embroidery designs and so make a personal statement.

When exploring a natural theme, a camera can be a useful tool for those of you who are not confident sketching from life. Photographs of landscapes, pets, farm and zoo animals, trees and forests can provide inspiration for a design. Try to take several shots of landscapes which interest you, taking each one from a different viewpoint, since you may be able to combine elements from each picture in your finished design. It is also a good idea to keep a notebook and write down the exact location and time of year when the photographs were taken. You will then be able to return at a different time of year and record any seasonal changes with your camera. This can be particularly valuable when investigating the design possibilities of a forest landscape or groups of trees. You may decide to design a whole set of embroideries, perhaps expressing nature's changes over each season of the year, or from month to month. Making detailed notes of colours and surface textures (for example, shiny, matt, smooth, granular) is also useful when you are selecting fabrics and threads for your project.

You may feel more at home adapting an existing image into a cross stitch design. Wildlife and countryside magazines are a good source of animal subjects, as are many illustrated children's books with their bold, simplified pictures. Travel magazines and glossy brochures may also spark off ideas. Carefully cut out any interesting pictures and file them away according to subject so that they are easy to find when you are ready to design. The experimenting chapter beginning on page 140 takes you through each stage of making your own cross stitch chart. Ready-charted designs, perhaps one intended for a Fair Isle sweater or piece of pictorial crochet, can be easily adapted for cross stitch and details of how to do this are given on page 143.

CRUNCHY
CARROT APRON

This cheerful apron featuring a trio of crisp, crunchy carrots would be a sure-fire winner with a certain cartoon character. The carrots are quick and easy to embroider in half cross stitch, cross stitch and back stitch.

MATERIALS

- White 130 cm (51 in) wide 18 count Damask Aida evenweave fabric (Zweigart E3239, colour 1)
- DMC stranded cotton in the following colours: oranges 608, 970, 972; green 906
- Tapestry needle size 24
- Tacking thread in a dark colour
- Sewing needle and pins
- Matching sewing thread
- Green bias binding or green cotton fabric
- Dressmaker's pattern paper
- Large embroidery hoop

MEASURING UP

The finished apron measures approximately 48 cm (19 in) wide by 76 cm (30 in) long. You will need a fabric rectangle of this size, plus a margin approximately 5 cm (2 in) wide all round.

PREPARING THE FABRIC

First, enlarge the apron pattern given on page 156 and cut a paper pattern from dressmaker's paper. Lay the paper pattern on the fabric rectangle and pin in position. Then tack round the edge of the pattern to mark the apron shape on the fabric. On the chart, the design covers an area 61 squares wide by 59 squares deep, and each coloured square represents one stitch worked over two vertical and two horizontal woven blocks of fabric. Mark the position of the embroidery by marking out a rectangular area 122 blocks wide by 118 blocks deep with lines of tacking. Here, the three carrots are placed centrally, about 5 cm (2 in) down from the top.

WORKING THE EMBROIDERY

1 Tack a vertical line through the centre of the rectangle taking care not to cross any vertical threads, then tack along the central horizontal line in the same way. Mark the centre of the chart with a soft pencil. Mount the fabric in the hoop (page 19).

906   972   970   608

THIS mouth-watering trio of carrots is embroidered with three strands of thread and uses a combination of cross stitch and half cross stitch outlined with back stitch. Start stitching the carrots at the centre of the design and work outwards, remembering that each square on the chart represents one stitch worked over two vertical and two horizontal fabric blocks.

2 Beginning in the centre and working outwards, work the carrots in half cross stitch (page 22) from the chart, using three strands of thread in the needle. Work the leaves in cross stitch (page 22), then outline the carrots with back stitch (page 22).

MAKING UP THE APRON

1 Press the embroidery lightly on the wrong side.
2 Cut out the apron along the tacked lines.
3 Bind the raw edges with ready-made bias binding (page 154) or make your own binding (page 153) from cotton fabric. Bind the armhole edges first, then along the top edge and finally round the remainder of the body of the apron.
4 Make the ties and neck strap by folding lengths of bias binding in half widthways and machine stitching all the way round close to the edge. Attach the ties and strap securely to the apron.

SWAN
CUSHION COVER

A square cushion cover makes the perfect setting for almost any pictorial cross stitch design. Here, a sedate white swan is sailing like a miniature galleon in and out of reeds at the river's edge. The whole tranquil picture is framed by a simply worked border of back stitch.

MATERIALS

- Blue 130 cm (51 in) wide 18 count Ainring even-weave fabric (Zweigart E3793, colour sky 503)
- DMC stranded cotton in the following colours: white; orange 740; turquoise 958, blues 340, 796, 809, 3746, 3747, 3760; greens 703, 907, 966; greys 413, 647
- Tapestry needle size 24
- Tacking thread in a dark colour
- Matching sewing thread and zip fastener
- Sewing needle and pins
- Ready-made cushion pad
- Large embroidery hoop or adjustable rectangular embroidery frame

MEASURING UP

Decide on the finished size of the cushion cover, bearing in mind that you will need sufficient fabric to make both the front and back. To the front, add at least a 10 cm (4 in) wide margin all round to allow you to mount the fabric in your hoop or frame. The plain back of each cover is made in two pieces joined by a central seam with a zip fastener inserted, so you will need to add a 5 cm (2 in) seam allowance, plus 2.5 cm (1 in) all round for turnings.

PREPARING THE FABRIC

Cut out the fabric for the front and mark the finished size onto the fabric with lines of tacking, taking care that the lines of stitches run between two rows of woven blocks of fabric. The design is worked in a central panel, leaving a wide margin of unworked fabric round the edge to create the effect of a frame. Tack a

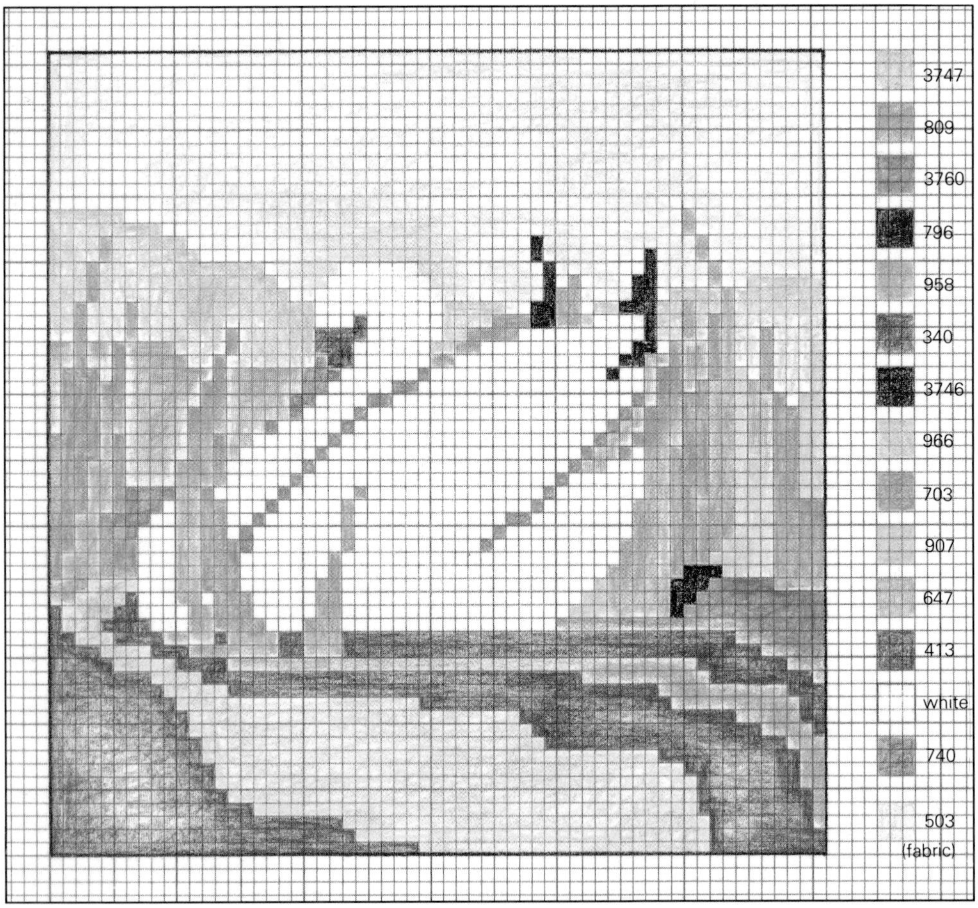

3747
809
3760
796
958
340
3746
966
703
907
647
413
white
740
503
(fabric)

THE DESIGN is worked on blue fabric, parts of which are left unstitched to form an integral part of the design. Create a partner for the swan by embroidering the goose chart on page 116 and framing it with back stitch in the same way.

vertical line through the centre of the fabric inside the tacked outline, taking care not to cross any vertical threads. Mark the central horizontal line in the same way and mark the centre of the chart with a soft pencil. Mount the fabric in the embroidery hoop or frame (pages 19–20).

WORKING THE EMBROIDERY

1 Begin working the design in cross stitch (page 22) at the centre of the fabric. Use three strands of thread and note that each coloured square on the chart represents one stitch worked over two vertical and two horizontal woven blocks of fabric.

2 Work a line of back stitch (page 22) all round the swan design to make a square panel. Work each stitch over two fabric blocks using two strands of blue 796.

3 Work further lines of back stitch in the same colour to create a mitred frame round the swan. Stitch from the corners of the panel towards the tacked line. Work each stitch diagonally across two vertical and two horizontal fabric blocks and take each line about 1.5 cm (½ in) over the tacking to avoid unsightly gaps in the lines of stitching when the cover is assembled.

MAKING UP THE CUSHION COVER

1 When all the embroidery has been completed, press lightly on the wrong side over a well-padded surface. Use a warm iron and take care not to press too hard and crush the stitching.

2 Cut out the fabric to the required size, allowing a margin of 2.5 cm (1 in) outside the tacked lines for the seam allowance on the front. Follow the illustrated instructions on page 155 for making up the cushion cover.

CHERRY
SHELF EDGING

Embroidered shelf edgings add an ornamental finish to open pine shelves and help show off a collection of pretty, flower-patterned plates and cream jugs. Here, the edgings are decorated with a repeat pattern of luscious red cherries.

MATERIALS

- White 110 cm (43 in) wide 11 count Pearl Aida even-weave fabric (Zweigart E3793, colour 1)
- Narrow white lace edging
- DMC stranded cotton in the following colours: reds 349, 816; greens 699, 703
- Tapestry needle size 24
- Tacking thread in a dark colour
- Matching sewing thread
- Sewing needle and pins
- Embroidery hoop or adjustable rectangular frame
- Self-adhesive fixing pads or double-sided adhesive tape for fixing the edging onto the shelves

MEASURING UP

Measure the length of the shelves and add 1.5 cm (½ in) to each end for turnings. The embroidery is worked in a band along one side of each strip, then the strip is folded in half lengthways with the raw edges tucked inside. The finished band is 5 cm (2 in) deep, so you will need twice this depth of fabric plus 2.5 cm (1 in) for turnings. Multiply the length measurement plus turnings by the number of shelves to calculate the amount of lace edging to buy.

PREPARING THE FABRIC

Mark the size of the shelf edging on the fabric with rows of tacking, positioning the strips side by side and allowing sufficient fabric between them for turnings. Mark the position of the embroidery with rows of tacking, then find the centre of each band and mark with a pin. Mount the fabric in the embroidery hoop or frame (pages 19–20).

WORKING THE EMBROIDERY

Work the repeat designs of cherries and leaves in cross stitch (page 22), starting at the centre of the band and working outwards. Use three strands of thread throughout and remember that each coloured square represents one cross stitch worked over one vertical and one horizontal woven block of fabric.

MAKING UP THE SHELF EDGING

1 Press lightly on the wrong side with a warm iron. Cut out the embroidered pieces.

2 Fold the strips in half lengthways, tucking in the raw edges and making sure that the band of embroidery is evenly spaced on the fabric and that the folds fall along the same rows of holes.

3 Pin together and tack in position, then work a row of machine stitching all round the edge of each strip. Slipstitch (page 152) the lace edging along the lower edge of each strip, neatly turning in about 1.5 cm (½ in) of lace at each end.

4 Give the strips a final light press, then attach to the shelves with either self-adhesive fixing pads or double-sided adhesive tape.

IDEAS TO INSPIRE

Many of the other designs illustrated in the pattern libraries can be used instead of the cherry border. The bee, fly, cow and strawberry borders on page 113 would look effective decorating the open shelves of a kitchen dresser, or you could embroider shelf edgings for your bathroom to match the butterfly-patterned towels on page 106.

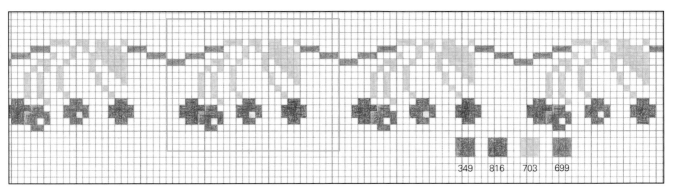

| 349 | 816 | 703 | 699 |

STITCHED in two shades of red and two of green, the cherry design is quick to work on 11 count evenweave fabric. When stitching this design, make sure you begin at the centre of each strip so that both ends of the pattern match. Fix the strips onto the front edge of your shelves with self-adhesive fixing pads or strips of double-sided adhesive tape, so that the fabric can be easily removed for laundering.

BUTTERFLY
TOWELS

 Decorate plain towels with rows of butterflies embroidered in soft pastel shades to add a touch of summer to your bathroom.

MATERIALS

- Cream 130 cm (51 in) wide 18 count Ainring even-weave fabric (Zweigart E3793, colour 264)
- Cream towels with a woven band at each end
- DMC stranded cotton in the following colours: pink 3733; mauve 210; turquoise 993; blues 334, 517, 798, 813; green 966

MEASURING UP

Measure the woven strip across your towels and add 1.5 cm (½ in) all round for turnings.

PREPARING THE FABRIC

Mark out the finished size of the bands on the fabric with rows of tacking, positioning the bands side by side and allowing sufficient fabric between them for turnings. Find the centre of each band and mark with a pin. Mount the fabric in the embroidery frame (page 20).

WORKING THE EMBROIDERY

Work the butterflies in cross stitch (page 22), starting at the centre of the band and working outwards. Use three strands of thread in a size 24 tapestry needle. Work the details in back stitch (page 22) using three strands of thread.

FINISHING THE TOWELS

Press lightly on the wrong side with a warm iron. Cut out the pieces, allowing 1.5 cm (½ in) of unworked fabric outside the tacked lines. Turn under the raw edges, pin in place and secure with slipstitch (page 152).

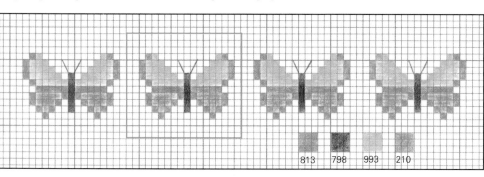

813 798 993 210

EACH COLOURED square represents one cross stitch worked over two vertical and two horizontal woven blocks of fabric. The coloured lines indicate rows of back stitch worked over two fabric blocks.

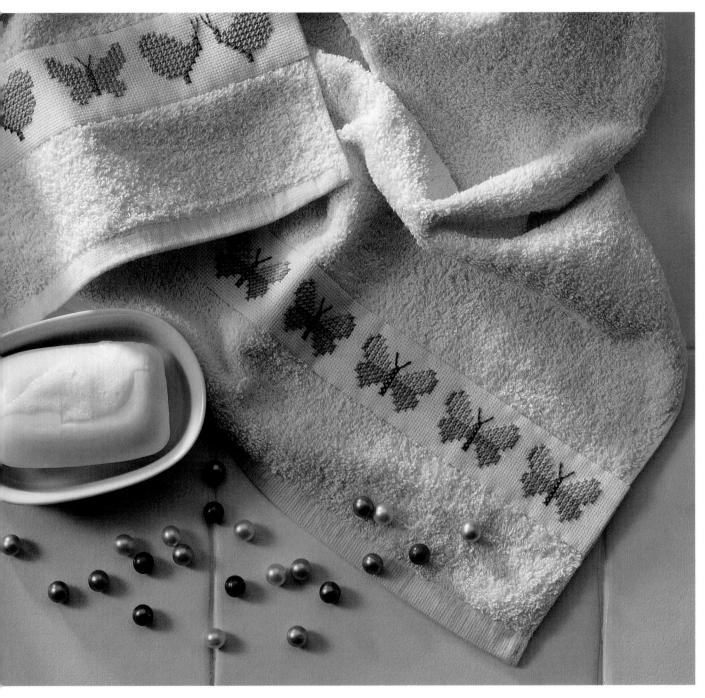

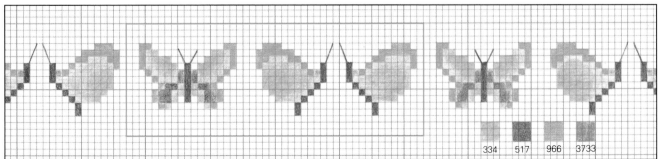

334	517	966	3733

SHELL
DRESSING TABLE MAT

 An embroidered mat is an attractive way of protecting the polished surface of a piece of furniture from scratches and knocks. The decoration can be as plain or as fancy as you like, with the colours chosen to match your furnishings. Here, two scallop shells in subtle shades of pink and rust are embroidered on white fabric, then the mat edges are finished off with a neat whipped border.

MATERIALS

- White 110 cm (43 in) wide 11 count Pearl Aida even-weave fabric (Zweigart E1007, colour 1)
- DMC stranded cotton in the following colours: pinks 3716, 3731, 3779; orange 722; light tan 3776; light rust 3778
- Tapestry needle size 24
- Tacking thread in a dark colour
- Sewing needle and pins
- Embroidery hoop

MEASURING UP

Measure the length and width of your dressing table or chest of drawers and decide on the finished size for the mat. Add a margin of at least 10 cm (4 in) wide all round to allow you to mount the fabric comfortably in the embroidery hoop while stitching. Mark the finished size of the mat on the fabric with lines of tacking.

PREPARING THE FABRIC

On the charts, each shell design covers an area 35 squares wide and 35 squares deep, and each coloured square represents one stitch worked over one woven block of fabric. Before you start to stitch, mark the position of the two shells on the mat by marking out two squares 35 blocks wide by 35 blocks deep with lines of tacking. Here, the shells are placed about 8 cm (3 in) from the corner, but you may prefer to alter their position.

WORKING THE EMBROIDERY

1 Tack a vertical line through the centre of each tacked square, taking care not to cross any vertical threads, then tack along the central horizontal lines in the same way. Mark the centre of the charts with a soft pencil.
2 Mount the fabric in the embroidery hoop (page 19),

and work the design in cross stitch (page 22) from the chart, using three strands of thread in the needle. Start stitching at the centre and work outwards, remembering that each square on the chart represents one cross stitch worked over one fabric block.

MAKING UP THE MAT

1 Press the embroidery lightly on the wrong side over a well-padded surface. Use a warm iron and take care not to press too hard and crush the stitching.
2 Cut the fabric to the required size, allowing a margin of 2.5 cm (1 in) outside the tacked lines for the hem allowance.

| 3731 | 3716 | 3778 | 722 | 3779 | 3776 |

3 Pin and tack a narrow double hem (page 152) round the dressing table mat, turning in the corners neatly. Make sure that the hemline fold runs neatly between two rows of fabric blocks. Also, take care to ensure that the shell motifs are an equal distance from the hem edge.

4 To complete the dressing table mat, secure the hem with a row of whipped back stitch (page 22) worked close to the turned-over edge. Work each back stitch over two woven blocks using three strands of pink 3779, then whip the stitched line with three strands of pink 3731. Press the hem edge lightly to make a crisp fold.

HERE, two shell motifs are worked on opposite corners of the mat, but you could equally well embroider one shell in each corner and work a second row of whipped back stitch just above the hem.

WORK EACH shell in the appropriate colours from the charts, then finish off the mat with a row of whipped back stitch worked in two shades of pink round the hem.

FISH BOWL
NURSERY PICTURE

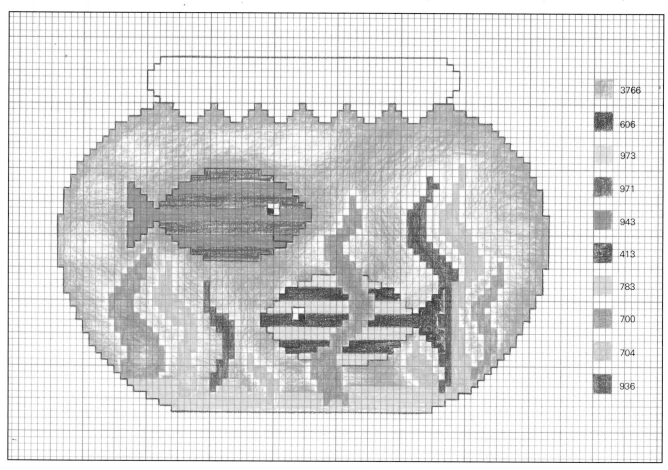 Jolly striped fish swimming in a fish bowl make a colourful nursery picture, suitable for either a boy or a girl. The design is quick and straightforward to stitch using a combination of cross stitch, half cross stitch and back stitch.

MATERIALS

- White 110 cm (43 in) wide 11 count Pearl Aida even-weave fabric (Zweigart E1007, colour 1)
- DMC stranded cotton in the following colours: red 606; orange 971; yellow 973; blue 3766; greens 700, 704, 936, 943; sand 783; grey 413
- Tapestry needle size 24
- Tacking thread in a dark colour
- Stitch and tear embroidery backing (optional)
- Sewing needle
- Adjustable rectangular embroidery frame or rectangular wooden stretcher
- Sturdy cardboard
- Strong linen carpet thread or very fine string

MEASURING UP

The embroidered area of the picture measures approximately 12.5 cm by 18 cm (5 in by 7 in). To this you will need to add at least 10 cm (4 in) all round to allow for mounting the fabric in a frame while you work the stitching, and to enable the finished embroidery to be laced round a piece of cardboard prior to framing. You may need to add a wider margin of fabric round the edge when working on a large embroidery frame or on a stretcher.

PREPARING THE FABRIC

Cut out the fabric and tack a vertical line through the centre of it, taking care not to cross any vertical threads. Tack the central horizontal line in the same way and mark the centre of the chart with a soft pencil. Mount the fabric in the embroidery frame or stretcher (page 20). If you are not an experienced stitcher, you may like to tack a piece of stitch and tear embroidery back-

	3766
	606
	973
	971
	943
	413
	783
	700
	704
	936

TO MAKE the picture into a special gift, add the child's name in cross stitch beneath the bowl.

OUTLINE THE shape of the fish bowl with a row of back stitches. This is indicated by grey lines on the chart.

stitch over one block of fabric. Pick out the details of the eye and mouth in the same way.

ing onto the wrong side of the fabric. This will give the fabric extra stability while you are stitching, and help to prevent puckering.

WORKING THE EMBROIDERY

1 Begin stitching at the centre of the design, noting that each coloured square on the chart represents one complete stitch worked over one woven block of fabric. Work the fish, weeds and sand in cross stitch (page 22) using three strands of thread in the needle throughout.

2 Next, embroider the water in half cross stitch (page 22). Outline the fish and the bowl in back stitch (page 22) using two strands of grey 413. Work each back

FINISHING THE PICTURE

1 When all the embroidery has been completed, carefully tear away the embroidery backing close to the stitching, if used. Press the embroidery lightly on the wrong side over a well-padded surface. Use a warm iron and take care not to press down too hard and crush the stitching.

2 Decide on the size of frame for the picture, then lace the embroidery (page 157) securely over a piece of sturdy card cut to the appropriate size. Use strong linen carpet thread or very fine string for the lacing.

3 Select a picture frame of your own choice from the several options available: a wooden stretcher, a simple clip frame or a conventional picture frame, with or without glass (page 157).

Natural Borders

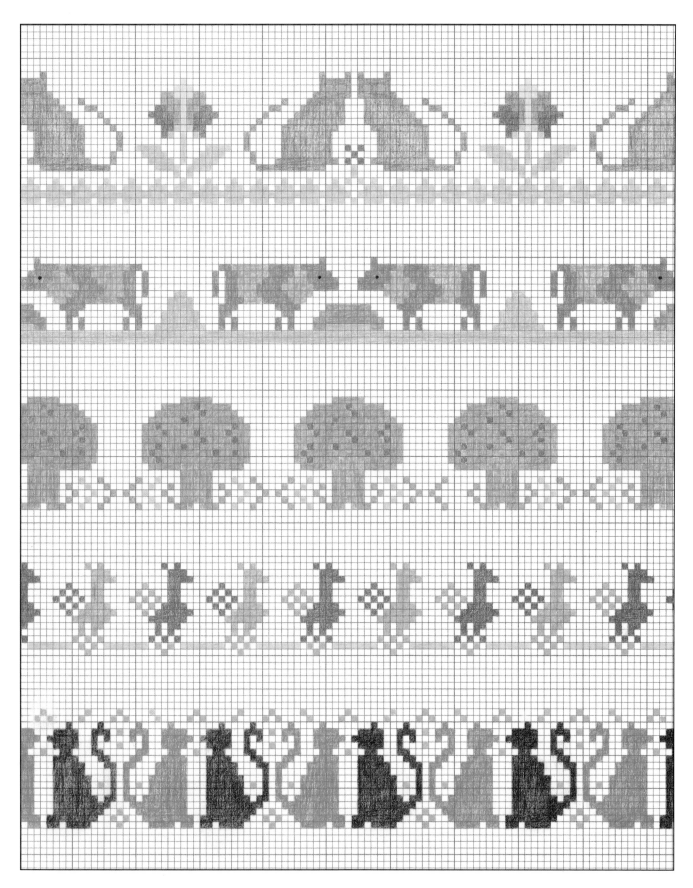

Natural Borders

Trees ... and a Dog

Cats . . . and a Rabbit

Birds and Butterflies

Sea Creatures and Butterflies

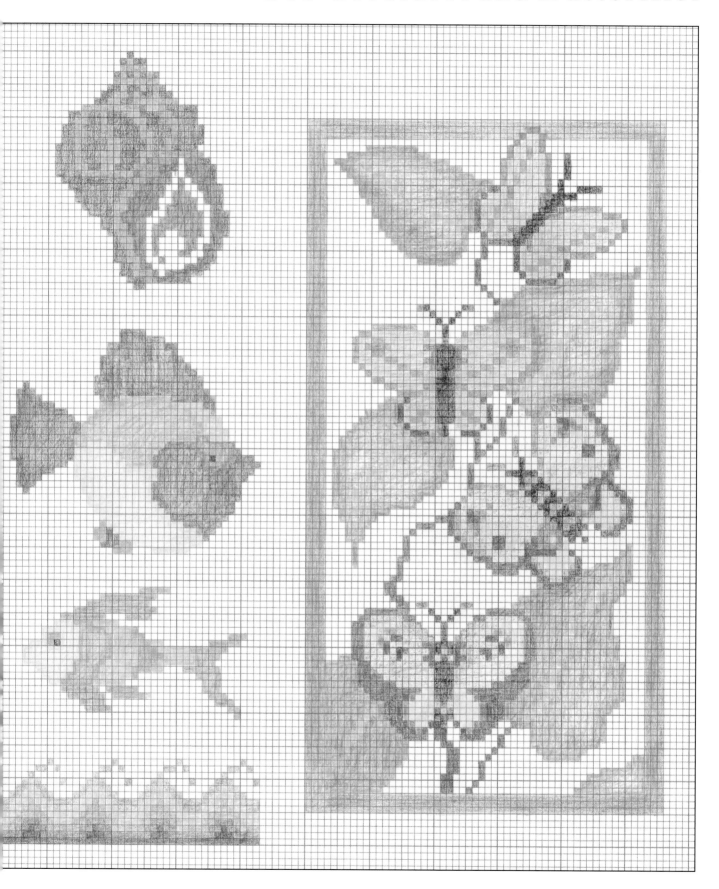

CHAPTER SEVEN

GEOMETRIC DESIGNS

INTRODUCTION

Embroidered geometric designs are visually bold and stylish, depending for their effect on being worked accurately and perfectly evenly. This type of design is composed predominantly of simple geometric forms such as rectangles, triangles and circles, together with straight and zig-zag lines. Some of the earliest decorative images were geometric, for example Ancient Greek key patterns, Celtic borders and all-over designs, Islamic and Indian lattices.

The corner motifs on the tablecloth on page 124 were inspired by the Art Deco style of design which was predominant during the 1920s and 1930s in both Europe and America. Art Deco designs are characterized by strongly stylized patterns with sharp edges and flat areas of clean, bright colours. The name 'Art Deco' was taken from an exhibition held in Paris during 1925, called the Exposition Internationale des Arts Décoratifs et Industriels Modernes, which brought this new style of design to the public. Art Deco was particularly popular in both decorative arts and interior decoration, but the term is also used to describe paintings, sculpture, domestic and industrial architecture of the period.

The tablecloth decoration is stitched in three strong colours: orange, green and dark blue, but you can alter these to coordinate with your own colour scheme, providing the thread colours you choose contrast strongly with your background fabric. The beauty of a corner design is that it can be used to decorate almost any size of tablecloth without having to be altered. Take care to measure and marked out the position of the motifs carefully on the fabric before you start stitching, ensuring that each motif is an identical distance away from the point of the corner.

Plain, ungathered café curtains with a scallop-shaped heading show off a geometric design well. The white curtain on page 133 is decorated with two identical narrow bands of red stitching, but you could substitute any of the other cross stitch borders shown in the pattern libraries, including the geometric ones on page 170. If you select a wide border, work a single band of pattern just above the hem. To achieve a completely different, less regular effect, work several small geometric motifs scattered at random across the lower third of the curtain, or embroider a group of stylized flower heads (page 44) just below the point where two scallops meet.

The pattern library at the end of this chapter contains a large selection of geometric borders (pages 134–135), complete with designs for corners. These designs can be substituted for the ones used in the sampler on page 128, or used in addition to create a long, narrow design. There are several square motifs on pages 136 and 137 which can be stitched at the centre of a cushion cover and then framed by one or more of the borders. Transfer your design onto graph paper to work out the arrangement of the design elements before you start to stitch (page 142), and work a small sample of each one on your chosen fabric to see how the thread colours react with each other. If you would like to use any of the other border charts which do not include corner designs, you will need a small rectangular mirror to work out the corner arrangement. The illustration on page 144 shows you how to do this.

Alternatively, repeat one of the square motifs to fill your cushion cover, perhaps varying the colour combinations from square to square, or working alternate squares in light and dark tones to make a chequerboard pattern. One of the designs on page 136 shows two square charts side by side. Both charts contain exactly the same design, but on the second one the dark and light areas have been filled in with the opposite colour. This design would be very effective arranged as a repeat pattern.

The pieced patchwork design which inspired the cot quilt on page 130 is typically American. Here, the top of the quilt is made all in one piece and divided up into squares of identical size with ties of embroidery thread to hold the layers of fabric, wadding and lining together. Alternate squares are decorated with simple blocks of cross stitch, using a range of bright pastel shades of thread. The blocks are arranged in sequence, but you could embroider each motif with a different colour.

There is no reason why you could not use separate pieces of fabric to make the quilt top, embroidering a design on each one and then stitching the squares together with a sewing machine. Disguise the resulting seams by working lines of running stitch along them to quilt the layers together instead of using thread ties. You could mix several pastel shades of fabric on the quilt top, providing each piece has exactly the same count. Instead of the geometric patchwork design, you could decorate the quilt squares with letters, flowers and animals to make a really individual gift for a new arrival. Choose suitable designs from the selection shown in the pattern libraries.

The pincushions on page 123 are an ideal project for a newcomer to cross stitch embroidery. The designs are quick and easy to stitch using just one colour of thread, and they all rely on brightly-coloured fabric for their visual impact. Working the three pincushion designs will allow you to practise stitching a simple repeat design from a chart, as well as executing the individual stitches neatly. This practice gives you valuable experience in following a chart, which will be useful when tackling the more complex projects in the book.

When stitching a geometric design, it is essential to stretch your background fabric in an embroidery hoop or rectangular frame. This will help keep the warp and weft of the fabric running at right angles to each other throughout the stitching process, so that the straight-edged shapes in the finished embroidery look neat, crisp and accurate. Remember to keep checking your stitching against the chart at regular intervals to identify and correct any mistakes. Always slacken off the tension on the hoop or frame at the end of each embroidery session and store your project wrapped in white tissue paper to keep it perfectly clean.

You may like to collect magazine cuttings of geometric patterns so that you can begin to design cross stitch projects of your own. Look for all-over patterns, borders and isolated motifs. Books on art and antiques, architectural ornament, textiles and interior design, particularly those illustrating the Art Deco period, will provide lots of inspiration. Look out for pottery by Clarice Cliff, Charlotte Rhead and Susie Cooper; rugs and poster designs by E McKnight Kauffer; silver by Georg Jensen; wrought iron and bronze by Edgar Brandt; jewellery by Van Cleef and Arpels, Cartier and Boucheron. Other sources of geometric design worth researching include illuminated manuscripts, Byzantine mosaics, decorated tiles, traditional American quilt and appliqué patterns, Amish quilts, abstract paintings and sculpture, Ancient Egyptian art, Fair Isle knitwear, flags and heraldic devices.

PATTERNED
PINCUSHIONS

 An embroidered pincushion makes a wonderful, quickly-stitched gift for a friend who loves needlecrafts. Make up one of these designs, then giftwrap the pincushion together with a pack of glass-headed pins, a thimble and ornamental embroidery scissors. You could stitch your friend's name or initials on the reverse, choosing small letters from the pattern library pages. All three geometric designs shown here can be worked over a larger area to make a cushion cover. Follow the instructions for making the scatter cushion with an all-over pattern on page 155.

MATERIALS

- Small pieces of dark blue, red and green 110 cm (43 in) wide 14 count Fine Aida evenweave fabric (Zweigart E3706, colours navy 589, Christmas red 954, holly green 670)
- DMC stranded cotton in white
- Tapestry needle size 24
- Tacking thread in a light colour
- Matching sewing threads
- Sewing needle and pins
- Polyester toy stuffing
- Knitting needle
- Embroidery hoop

MEASURING UP

You will need one piece of fabric for the front and one for the back of each pincushion you make. The finished sizes of the pincushions are as follows: red – 13 cm by 11.5 cm (5 in by 4½ in), green – 11 cm (4¼ in) square, blue – 9 cm by 8 cm (3½ in by 3 in). You will need to add 1.5 cm (½ in) all round to both front and back pieces for the seam allowance, plus a sufficiently wide margin all round the front pieces to allow you to mount the fabric in the hoop.

PREPARING THE FABRIC

The pincushions feature all-over patterns and they are all made by the same method. First tack a vertical line through the centre of the fabric, taking care not to cross any vertical threads. Mark the central horizontal line in the same way and mark the centre of the chart with a soft pencil. Mount the fabric in the embroidery hoop (page 19).

WORKING THE EMBROIDERY

1 Begin working in cross stitch (page 22) at the centre of the fabric using three strands of thread and noting that each square on the chart represents one stitch worked over two vertical and two horizontal woven blocks of fabric.

2 Complete stitching the area shown inside the light blue lines on the chart, then outline the design in back stitch worked in three strands of thread over two fabric blocks. When you reach the end of each side, take a diagonal back stitch over two vertical and two horizontal blocks to round off the corner.

MAKING UP THE PINCUSHIONS

1 Press the embroidery lightly on the wrong side with a warm iron. Cut the front to the required size, allowing a margin of 1.5 cm (½ in) all round for the seam allowance.

2 Place the front and back pieces together with right sides facing. Pin and tack together, then machine stitch twice round the edges just outside the row of white back stitch with matching thread. Leave an unstitched section along one side.

3 Clip the corners (page 155) and turn the pincushion right side out, taking care to push each corner out gently with the knitting needle.

4 Stuff the pincushion firmly with polyester toy stuffing, using the point of the knitting needle to help manoeuvre stuffing into each corner.

5 Slipstitch (page 152) the opening closed.

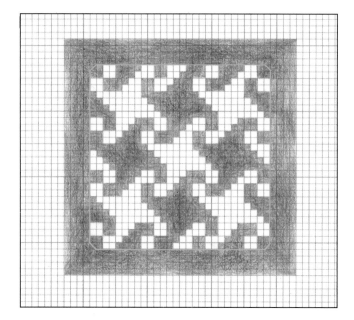

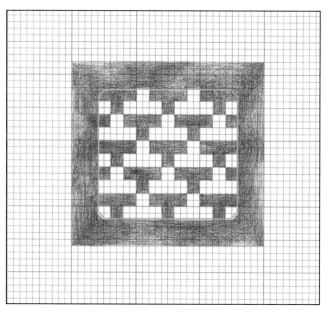

IN DAYS GONE BY, pins were so expensive and difficult to obtain that special cushions filled with sand or sawdust were made to house them. By the eighteenth century, ornamental pincushions were often given as gifts, especially Christening pincushions made from white satin. These were decorated with pins to make a pattern, and spelt out the name and birth date of the child. Victorian patchwork pincushions often had a motto spelt out in pins.

ART DECO
TABLECLOTH AND NAPKINS

 Corner motifs in the angular Art Deco style of the 1930s add splashes of colour to a formal tablecloth. A fragment of the design is repeated at one corner of matching napkins.

MATERIALS

- White 130 cm (51 in) wide 18 count Ainring even-weave fabric (Zweigart E3793, colour 1)
- DMC stranded cotton in the following colours: white; orange 971; blue 796; green 700
- Tapestry needle size 24
- Tacking thread in a dark colour
- Matching sewing thread
- Sewing needle and pins
- Large and small embroidery hoops

MEASURING UP

TABLECLOTH:

The corner designs can be used to decorate any size of square or rectangular tablecloth, but remember that the width of the fabric you choose will limit the size of the finished cloth. To make a cloth to fit a particular table, first measure the length and width of the table top. Decide how far you want the cloth to hang down over the edge of the table and add twice this measurement to each of the table top measurements. Finally, add 7 cm (2¾ in) to each measurement for the hem allowance.

NAPKINS:

Napkins are usually square, varying in size from small tea napkins of 30 cm (12 in) to large dinner napkins of 60 cm (24 in). Decide on a size to suit you, adding 2 cm (¾ in) all round for the hem allowance. However, when using this type of evenweave fabric, a good all-purpose size for a napkin is 38 cm (15 in) square. Lengths of 130 cm (51 in) width fabric can be divided evenly for napkins of this size, with sufficient left for hem allowances after trimming away the selvedges. From a 90 cm (36 in) length of fabric, you will be able to cut a set of six napkins.

EMBROIDER a large Art Deco motif in each corner of the tablecloth and the small motif in one corner of each napkin to make a matching set of table linen. Repeat four of the tablecloth motifs in a block to make a stylish design for a square cushion cover.

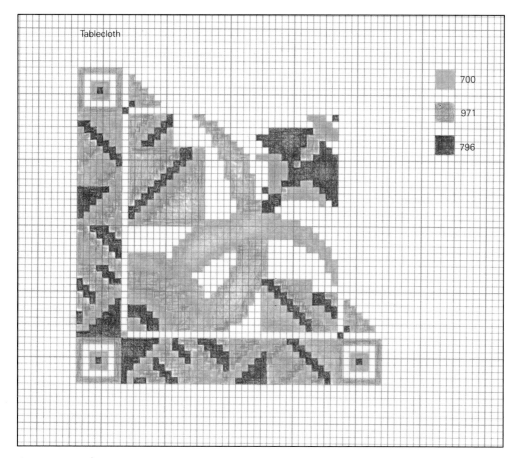

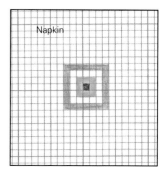

ON BOTH CHARTS, *each coloured square represents one complete cross stitch worked over two vertical and two horizontal fabric blocks. Work both designs using three strands of thread.*

PREPARING THE FABRIC

TABLECLOTH:

Tack a guideline round the cloth 10 cm (4 in) from the position of the finished edge. On the chart, the design covers an area 48 squares wide and 48 squares deep, with each coloured square representing one stitch worked over two vertical and two horizontal woven blocks of fabric. At each corner of the guideline, mark out an area 96 blocks square with lines of tacking to accommodate the corner motif.

NAPKIN:

Mark out an area 14 blocks square, placing it 6 cm (2½ in) from the corner.

WORKING THE EMBROIDERY

TABLECLOTH:

1 Tack a vertical line through the centre of each square, taking care not to cross any vertical threads, then tack along the central horizontal line in the same way. Mark the centre of the chart with a soft pencil.

2 Mount the fabric in the large embroidery hoop (page 19), and work the design in cross stitch (page 22) from the chart, using three strands of thread in the needle throughout. Start stitching at the centre and work outwards, remembering that each square on the chart represents one cross stitch worked over two vertical and two horizontal fabric blocks.

NAPKIN:

Begin stitching at the edge of the tacked square.

MAKING UP THE TABLECLOTH AND NAPKINS

1 Press the embroideries lightly on the wrong side.

2 Fold under 2 cm (¾ in) round the raw edge of the tablecloth, then a further 5 cm (2 in) to make an uneven hem (page 152), and mitre the corners (page 153). Make sure that the hemline fold runs neatly between two rows of fabric blocks. Hand sew the hem (page 152).

3 Pin and tack a narrow double hem (page 152) round the raw edge of each napkin, turning in the corners neatly. Secure the hems with hemming stitch.

4 Work a row of back stitch (page 22) round both the cloth and napkins, positioning each row just below the turned-over edge of the hem. Use three strands of white thread and work each stitch over two or three fabric blocks.

DECORATIVE
BORDERS

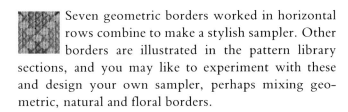 Seven geometric borders worked in horizontal rows combine to make a stylish sampler. Other borders are illustrated in the pattern library sections, and you may like to experiment with these and design your own sampler, perhaps mixing geometric, natural and floral borders.

MATERIALS

- Grey 110 cm (43 in) wide 14 count Fine Aida even-weave fabric (Zweigart E3706, colour pewter 713)
- DMC stranded cotton in the following colours: pink 3607; lavender 554; mauves 340, 3746; turquoises 958, 993; blues 312, 798, 809
- Tapestry needle size 24
- Tacking thread in a dark colour
- Stitch and tear embroidery backing (optional)
- Sewing needle
- Adjustable rectangular embroidery frame or rectangular wooden stretcher
- Clip frame 40 cm × 50 cm (16 in × 20 in)
- Sheet of paper 40 cm × 50 cm (16 in × 20 in) to match one of the thread colours

MEASURING UP

The embroidered area of the picture measures approximately 23 cm × 20 cm (9 in × 8 in). To this you will need to add at least 10 cm (4 in) all round to allow for mounting the fabric in a frame to work the stitching. You may need to add a wider margin of fabric round the edge when working on a large embroidery frame or on a stretcher, or if you prefer to have the sampler framed in a different way.

PREPARING THE FABRIC

Cut out the fabric and tack a vertical line through the centre of the fabric, taking care not to cross any vertical threads. Mark the central horizontal line in the same way and mark the centre of the chart with a soft pencil. Mount the fabric in the embroidery frame or stretcher (page 20). If you are not an experienced stitcher, you may like to tack a piece of stitch and tear embroidery backing on to the wrong side of the fabric. This will give the fabric extra stability while you are stitching, and help to prevent puckering.

WORKING THE EMBROIDERY

1 Begin stitching at the centre of the design, noting that each coloured square on the chart represents one complete stitch worked over two vertical and two hori-

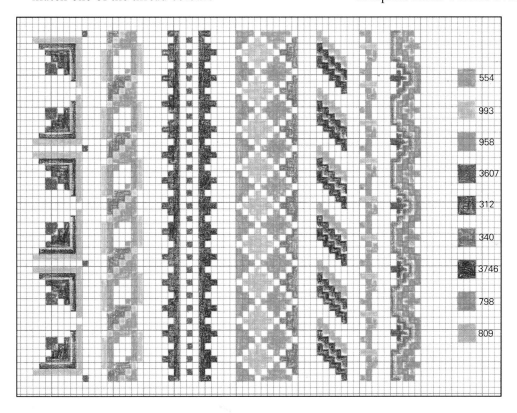

	554
	993
	958
	3607
	312
	340
	3746
	798
	809

BEFORE you begin to work from the chart, you will need to turn the book to your right so that the chart is the correct way up. Check with the photograph on pages 128 and 129.

zontal woven blocks of fabric. Work the borders in cross stitch (page 22) using three strands of thread in the needle throughout.

2 Work carefully from the chart, stopping at intervals to check that the individual components are spaced correctly and that the top diagonal of each stitch faces in the same direction.

FINISHING THE PICTURE

1 When all the embroidery has been completed, carefully trim away the embroidery backing, if used. Cut close to the outside of the stitched area with a sharp pair of embroidery scissors. Press the embroidery lightly on the wrong side over a well-padded surface. Use a warm iron and take care not to press down too hard.

2 Trim off the surplus fabric round the edge of the embroidery leaving a margin of 5 cm (2 in) at the top, 7.5 cm (3 in) at the bottom and 4 cm (1½ in) at each side. Take care to cut each edge along the same row of holes in the fabric.

3 Fringe each side by gently teasing out the threads one at a time with a tapestry needle until you have about 6 mm (¼ in) of fringe all the way round the edge. Press again from the wrong side.

4 Remove the clips from the frame and lay the backing board right side up on a flat surface. Cover this with the coloured paper, then carefully lay the sampler on top. Check the position of the sampler and make sure that even margins of paper are showing at each side of the fabric.

5 Clean both sides of the glass to remove dust and fingermarks, then lay the glass on top of the sampler. Attach the clips. This type of frame is suitable for designs without too much solid detail, such as this, since the glass presses down on the stitches and flattens them. However, you will need to keep the picture well dusted to prevent dirt penetrating under the glass and eventually spoiling the fabric.

IDEAS TO INSPIRE

This selection of geometric borders can be used in a variety of ways for cross stitch embroidery. Work one or more designs together to make a wide band across a tablemat (page 60), or decorate the ends of a runner (page 52); stitch a single border to coordinate hand and bath towels (page 106); embroider a deep border round a square or rectangular cloth, altering the design to fit round the corners with the help of a small hand mirror (page 144).

HERE, *the borders are stitched in harmonious shades of pink, mauve, turquoise and blue, giving a restful feel to the design. You could choose a range of strong, bright colours instead to create a bolder, more dynamic effect. Alternatively, contrast white, pale grey, cream and lemon yellow threads against a black, navy blue or deep green background.*

PATCHWORK
COT QUILT

 Embroidered blocks alternate with plain blocks to make this cot quilt with a patchwork design. The layers are held together by thread ties.

MATERIALS

- Cream 110 cm (43 in) wide 14 count Fine Aida even-weave fabric (Zweigart E3706, colour 264)
- DMC stranded cotton in the following colours: pinks 604, 3708; mauve 554; lavender 340; yellows 725, 726; turquoise 964; blues 597, 3755; green 954; cream 712
- Medium-weight polyester wadding
- Patterned fabric for binding and lining

PREPARING THE FABRIC

Each block measures 11 cm (4¼ in) square. You will need a rectangle of fabric in multiples of this size plus a 10 cm (4 in) wide margin all round. Each block covers an area 30 squares wide and 30 squares deep, and each coloured square represents one stitch worked over two vertical and two horizontal blocks of fabric. Mark the position of the blocks by tacking a series of squares 60 blocks wide by 60 blocks deep across the fabric.

WORKING THE EMBROIDERY

Find the centre of the first embroidered block and mark with a pin. Mark the centre of the chart with a soft pencil. Mount the fabric in an embroidery hoop (page 19). Work the design in cross stitch (page 22), using three strands of thread in a size 24 tapestry needle. Repeat on alternate blocks.

MAKING UP THE QUILT

1 Press the embroidery lightly on the wrong side with a warm iron. Trim off surplus fabric leaving a margin of 2.5 cm (1 in) round the edge.

2 Sandwich the wadding between the embroidered front and the lining, and tack the layers together at intervals across the quilt and round the edge. Using six strands of cream 712, take two small stitches at the corner of each block, leaving the thread ends on the front of the fabric. Tie ends securely in a knot and trim to the same length.

3 Make lengths of bias binding (page 153) to match the lining and bind the edges, mitring the corners.

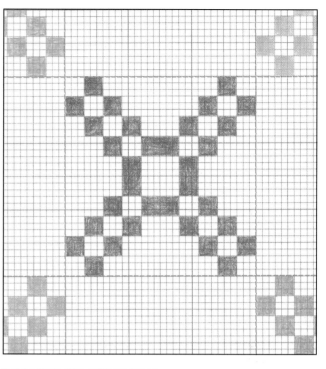

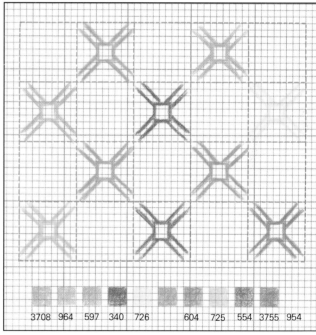

| 3708 | 964 | 597 | 340 | 726 | | 604 | 725 | 554 | 3755 | 954 |

THE QUILT *can easily be made larger or smaller by simply adding or subtracting blocks. Plan out your alternative design on graph paper (page 143) before you start to stitch.*

THE DIAGRAM *above shows how to repeat the embroidered blocks across the quilt in colour sequence, alternating them with unstitched blocks.*

CAFÉ
CURTAIN BORDER

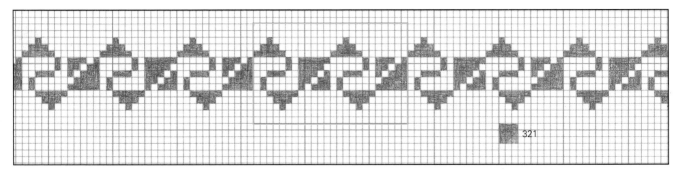

Make this stylish café curtain to hide an unsightly view or give you privacy where a window is constantly overlooked. The bands of geometric pattern can be stitched in any colour to coordinate with your furnishings, and the curtain is finished with a faced, scallop-shaped heading.

MATERIALS

- White 130 cm (51 in) wide 18 count Damask Aida evenweave fabric (Zweigart E3239, colour 1)
- DMC stranded cotton in red, 321
- Tapestry needle size 24
- Tacking thread in a dark colour
- Sewing needle and pins
- Matching sewing thread
- Dressmaker's pattern paper
- Embroidery hoop
- Narrow brass pole with fittings

MEASURING UP

Flat café curtains require less fabric than gathered curtains: just the width of the window recess, plus 5 cm (2 in) ease and 2.5 cm (1 in) for each side hem. Measure from the pole to the windowsill and add 10 cm (4 in) for the top turning and base hem. You will also need a strip of fabric the same width and 20 cm (8 in) deep to make the scalloped facing. Add at least 10 cm (4 in) to the width of the curtain to allow you to mount the design area in the hoop while stitching.

PREPARING THE FABRIC

Mark the finished edge of the curtain with a row of tacking 20 cm (8 in) from the raw edge. Mark the position of the two bands of embroidery with tacking, the first to come 12.5 cm (5 in) above the finished edge and the second 23 cm (9 in) above the same edge. These lines mark the bottom of each band.

WORKING THE EMBROIDERY

1 Mark the centre of both bands with a pin or several tacking stitches. Mark the centre of the chart with a soft pencil.

2 Mount the fabric in the hoop (page 19), and work the design in cross stitch (page 22) from the chart, using four strands of thread in the needle throughout. Start stitching at the centre of each band and work outwards, remembering that each square on the chart represents one cross stitch worked over three vertical and three horizontal fabric blocks.

MAKING UP THE CAFÉ CURTAIN

1 Press the embroidery lightly on the wrong side over a well-padded surface. Use a warm iron and take care not to press too hard and crush the stitching.

2 Cut away the surplus fabric at the sides, leaving a 2.5 cm (1 in) hem allowance.

3 Pin and tack a narrow double hem (page 152) at each side, making sure that the hemline fold runs neatly between two rows of fabric blocks. Machine stitch close to the turned over edge.

4 Follow the illustrated instructions given on page 156 for how to make the scalloped heading at the top of the curtain.

5 Hang the curtain to check that the hem is in the correct position. Turn under 1.5 cm (½ in) along the lower edge of the curtain, then a further 7.5 cm (3 in) to make a deep hem. Pin, tack and secure with machine stitching or hemming stitch (page 152).

WORK THE pattern bands outwards from the centre of the curtain, taking care that the design on each band begins and ends in the same place.

CAFÉ CURTAINS look best against a small window. Here, a brass pole with matching clips is fixed across the window recess to hold the curtain.

321

Borders and Corners

Borders and Corners

Geometric Motifs

Geometric Motifs

Geometric Repeat Patterns

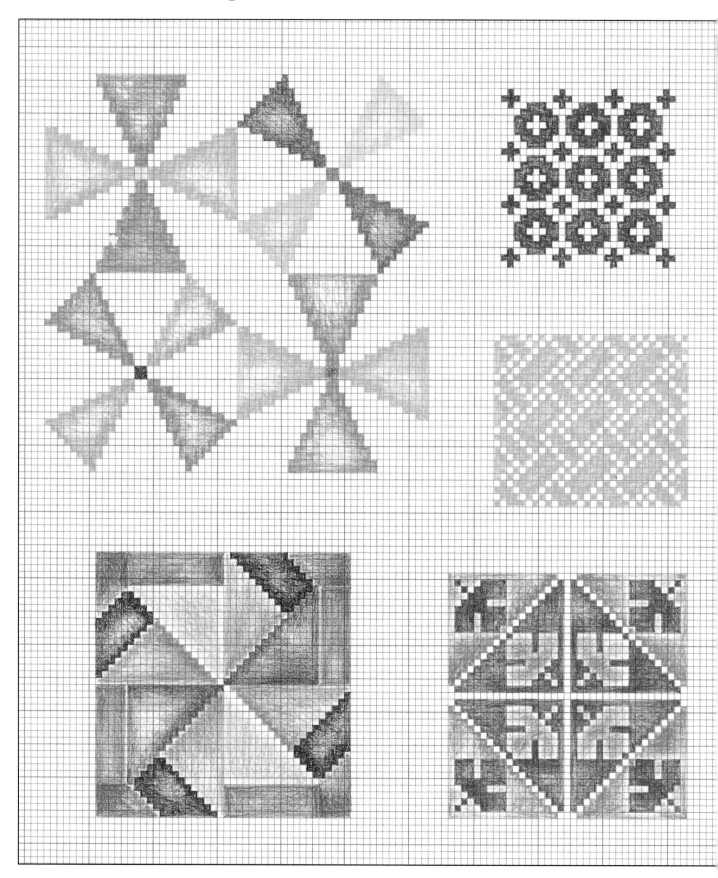

Geometric Repeat Patterns

CHAPTER EIGHT

EXPERI-MENTING

MAKING YOUR OWN CHARTS

Cross stitch is probably the most popular embroidery technique which is worked by counting fabric threads to calculate the position of each stitch. These techniques are called counted thread embroidery, and this term also includes needlepoint, pattern darning, blackwork and bargello or Florentine embroidery. Designs for cross stitch are almost always charted, with each different area indicated by the appropriate colour or by a range of symbols. The design is worked on evenweave fabric by following the chart square by square, and at the same time counting the threads or blocks in the fabric. It is usual to begin at the centre of a design and work outwards, remembering that each square on the chart represents one stitch.

Designing a chart is the starting point when embroidering your own, unique piece of cross stitch, and this can be a truly rewarding experience. The subject of the embroidery can be anything you choose, perhaps a sketch or large photograph of your home, family, pet dog, cat or bird, and the design can be worked in any combination of colours you like. If you are not skilled at drawing and designing, select a ready-made image and adapt that to make your chart. Suggestions for source material are given in the opening pages of each chapter, but remember that there is a wealth of pictures and patterns all around you, in magazines, illustrated books, on wrapping paper, greetings cards, printed dress and furnishing fabrics, and they are all waiting to be adapted into cross stitch designs. Your local photocopy shop may have a photocopying machine which can enlarge an image, and this facility is particularly useful when your chosen design source is too small.

One of the most useful aids when making your own chart is a supply of graphed tracing paper. This is heavy tracing paper with a ready-printed grid, and it is usually stocked by shops selling artist's materials. It is available in pads and single sheets with a sepia, black or red grid and you should buy the variety with a large grid divided into tenths of an inch. If you are unable to obtain this type of paper, use good quality plain tracing paper instead and divide this up into a small-scale grid using a ruler and black waterproof marker with a fine point. You will also need ordinary graph paper with an identical grid, a selection of coloured felt tip pens or pencils, typist's correction fluid and masking tape. You can colour in your charts using gouache, choosing a range of basic colours and mixing them.

HOW TO MAKE A CROSS STITCH CHART

1 Lay a piece of graphed tracing paper over the picture and secure with pieces of masking tape. Draw round the shapes in the picture by carefully following the squares on the tracing paper with a black felt tip pen with a fine point. You can begin to simplify your design at this stage, perhaps leaving out one or two small elements and making the outline less fussy.

2 Transfer the shapes from the tracing paper to a piece of graph paper, following your design square by square. Use the black pen and do not worry if you make a mistake – it can be easily corrected with typist's correction fluid. At this point, you may decide to eliminate parts of the design, alter a curve to make a nicer

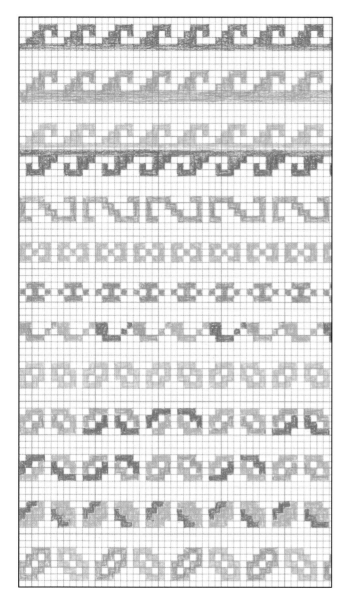

THE PATTERNS on ethnic knitted and woven textiles can often inspire a cross stitch design. Here, 12 narrow bands of pattern have been isolated from a group of Peruvian hats and shown in chart form, ready for you to begin stitching.

ADAPTING EXISTING CHARTS

You can easily adapt ready-charted designs, whether those shown in the pattern libraries, charts for Fair Isle and picture knitting or needlepoint charts. You may, for example, want to make an all-over design or border from a single motif, such as the pansy on page 43.

1 Draw several identical pansy motifs on graph paper and cut them out separately, leaving a margin of one square all round each motif. Lay the motifs on a large sheet of graph paper and begin moving them around until you are happy with the arrangement. Try arranging the motifs in neat vertical and horizontal rows, exactly as though you were placing one motif on each square of a chessboard. This arrangement is the most simple type of repeat design and often looks very attractive, especially when the motifs are complex.

2 Next, move the vertical row of motifs at one side down slightly, so that the centre of each motif on this row lines up neatly between two motifs on the adjacent row. Repeat the movement on every alternate row. The repeat you have now created is called a half-drop repeat.

3 When you are happy with the arrangement, stick the motifs in position using double-sided adhesive tape or paper glue, and make sure that the gaps between the motifs are identical.

Use this technique of drawing and cutting out each element of a design to create your own borders, pictures and samplers, and for working out the spacing between individual words or letters. You can select just one element of a large, ready-charted design and isolate it to make a small design. If you are designing a continuous border to stretch right round the edge of a piece of fabric, work out the corner design with the help of a small mirror, following the diagram on page 144.

EXPERIMENTING WITH SCALE

When your chart is complete, the next step is to choose a suitable fabric for the background. Evenweave fabric comes in various counts (the number of threads or woven blocks which can be stitched in 2.5 cm/1 in of fabric). The weight varies from fine to coarse, with fine

shape, or move some of the elements to a different position.

3 When you are happy with the shapes and arrangement, colour in the different areas of the design with felt tip pens or coloured pencils. Alternatively, use symbols such as crosses, slashes and spots to represent each colour.

4 Finally, make a colour key at the side of your chart by filling in a small square with each colour of pen or pencil you have used. When you have decided on a pleasing colour scheme, write the code number of each shade of thread next to the appropriate square.

5 Take your chart with you when selecting and purchasing threads in case you need to make changes to your colour scheme.

fabrics having more threads or blocks to each 2.5 cm (1 in) than the coarse ones.

Begin by counting the number of horizontal and vertical squares on your chart. Supposing your chart is 40 squares wide and 60 squares deep and you are thinking of stitching the design on fabric with a count of 10 blocks to 2.5 cm (1 in). If you allow each square on the chart to represent one block, the finished, embroidered design will cover an area 10 cm by 15 cm (4 in by 6 in).

MAKE A corner design to suit your border chart by using a mirror angled at 45° and charting the reversed image.

alternating between them at random, and create a really unusual interpretation of a charted design.

MAKING A SAMPLE LIBRARY

Before beginning a piece of cross stitch embroidery, it is a good idea to stitch a small section of the design to make sure you are happy with your chosen combination of fabric and threads. A small sample of stitching, about 5 cm (2 in) square, is usually sufficient to gauge the finished result. Keep all your samples, then stick or staple each one onto a 13 cm by 20 cm (5 in by 8 in) file card, noting down the details of fabric and threads used, together with any other relevant information. This size leaves plenty of space for written notes and allows you to file your samples neatly away in a card index box.

When working the same design on finer fabric with a count of 20 blocks to 2.5 cm/1 in, your finished embroidery will be much smaller, at 5 cm by 7.5 cm (2 in by 3 in). By allowing each square to represent three vertical and horizontal blocks instead of one, the design will come out much larger and cover an area 3 × 40 threads by 3 × 60 threads (120 by 180 threads, measuring 30 cm by 45 cm/ 12 in by 18 in).

This way of changing the size of any design by simply choosing a different fabric count can be very useful when you need to enlarge or reduce an image. Instead of having to redraw the chart, you can easily choose another fabric.

Often, you will want to stitch several samples just to try out the effects of unusual colour schemes, or to see how a design looks when worked on different counts of evenweave fabric. Work the same simple design several times in different colourways, choosing a fine linen with 24 threads to 2.5 cm (1 in), Aida fabric with a count of 14 blocks to 2.5 cm (1 in) and a coarse fabric with 8 threads to 2.5 cm (1 in). Experiment with different thicknesses of thread, using three strands of stranded cotton when working on the fine linen; Persian or tapestry wool for the coarse fabric.

Many designs, especially those with complicated geometric patterns, look best stitched in just one colour such as dark red or blue on cream, while others only come to life when using lots of colours.

DISTORTING A CHARTED DESIGN

A design can be distorted widthways or lengthways, and distortion can produce interesting results, especially on fabrics which are woven in regular blocks.

For example, when you have a chart showing a long, narrow flower, you could work each cross stitch over a rectangular area one block wide by two blocks deep instead of over the usual square. This will have the result of elongating the flower still further. Then try working the same flower again, but this time distort the design in the opposite direction by working each cross stitch over a rectangle three blocks wide and one block deep. You could combine these two techniques,

FREESTYLE CROSS STITCH

Random cross stitch can be worked freely on a fabric which is not evenly woven. You do not need to make a chart, and this technique works particularly well when the fabric has been prepared by painting or dyeing

MODERN LASER copiers offer a technique called pixelisation, which splits up a coloured image into hundreds of squares. This technique can be very useful when designing your own chart, but you will need to simplify the results considerably before starting to stitch.

(page 148). Work cross stitch in this way to create a unique picture, wall hanging or cushion cover, perhaps selecting a fabric for the background which has a printed or woven pattern. Working cross stitch without counting the fabric threads gives a totally different look, and the effect is free and spontaneous. You can use any kind of thread you like, from traditional embroidery threads, such as stranded cotton and tapestry wool, to fine ribbon and multi-coloured knitting yarns, but remember that thick and textured threads can only be pulled through fabric which has a loose, open weave.

Highlight some of the details by working groups of French knots (page 23) in-between the cross stitches, or add texture and sparkle by applying beads and sequins. French knots look luxurious when worked in stranded pure silk thread, since this is shiny and the surfaces of the stitches catch and reflect light. Stranded silk thread can also be mixed in tiny amounts with cotton thread to add a subtle lustre. When shading, try mixing one strand of silk with two or three of stranded cotton.

TRANSFERRING AND STITCHING A FREE DESIGN

1 Begin by drawing (or tracing) and colouring in your design. You then need to transfer the outlines of the largest areas onto the fabric. Do this by tracing round them on thin tracing paper or kitchen greaseproof. Pin the tracing to the right side of your fabric and tack through both tracing paper and fabric, working along all the lines. Score along the stitched lines with a tapestry needle and carefully tear away the paper to leave the tacked lines.

2 Begin stitching inside the tacked shapes using the appropriate thread colours. Do not worry about trying to work the crosses evenly; instead vary the size and angle of your stitches, overlapping them to build up areas of texture or spacing them out to let parts of the fabric show through.

WORKING CROSS STITCH DESIGNS ON CANVAS

Embroidery on canvas is called either needlepoint or canvaswork (never call it 'tapestry', since this is a term used for a type of weaving). Needlepoint produces a versatile embroidered fabric which, when worked in the appropriate threads, is extremely hard wearing and can be used to cover chair seats and stool tops as well as making lovely cushion covers, pictures, purses and small items. Canvas is constructed to form a regular grid like evenweave fabric, and it also has a specified count.

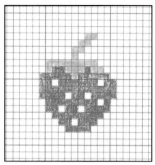

SIX WAYS to interpret a charted strawberry. Clockwise from top right:

1 Each stitch over two vertical and horizontal woven blocks

2 Back stitch

3 Distorted widthways

4 Half cross stitch

5 Distorted lengthways

6 Each stitch over one woven block.

Canvas is woven from stiffened cotton threads and these are usually completely hidden by the embroidery.

A cross stitch chart can be worked square by square on canvas without requiring adaptation, but remember that you will need to embroider the background as well as the design areas. Cross stitch (page 22) is popular, but many other canvas stitches can be used, depending on the effect you require. Square-shaped stitches are particularly good to use when working from a cross stitch chart, and a selection (reversed cushion stitch, crossed corners cushion stitch, chequer stitch, leviathan stitch, rice stitch, woven cross stitch and Rhodes stitch) are shown on pages 24–25.

There is a wide range of threads available for needlepoint, and you should try to match the weight of your embroidery thread to that of the canvas so that the grid is adequately covered by the stitching. Crewel, Persian and tapestry wood are available in a good colour range and are all hard wearing and suitable for use on an upholstered article. Stranded, pearl and soft embroidery cottons are used on a finer grade of canvas to work pictures and the whole range of small items such as purses and pincushions.

Always work with your canvas stretched in a rectangular frame, either the adjustable type (page 20) or a wooden stretcher (page 20), since this will help prevent the canvas pulling out of shape too much. An embroidery hoop is not suitable for needlepoint. When all the design has been embroidered, block the canvas to remove any distortions from both the stitching and the canvas grid. You will need a flat piece of soft, unpainted wood or blockboard 2 cm (¾ in) thick covered with polythene, rustproof tacks, a small hammer and a water spray or sponge. The wood should be at least 5 cm (2 in) larger all round than the canvas.

BLOCKING NEEDLEPOINT

1 Lay the needlepoint on the polythene with the right side facing upwards. Moisten the canvas with the spray or damp sponge, but do not saturate it. When there is a selvedge along one side of the canvas, cut several nicks in this edge so the canvas will stretch evenly.

2 Hammer a tack into the centre of the unworked margin at the top of the canvas, stretch the canvas gently downwards and hammer in a tack at the centre of the lower edge, making sure that the vertical canvas threads are straight. Repeat along the two remaining sides, this time making sure that warp and weft threads are at right angles to each other.

3 Working outwards from the centre of each side,

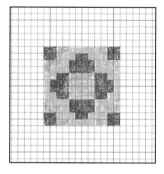

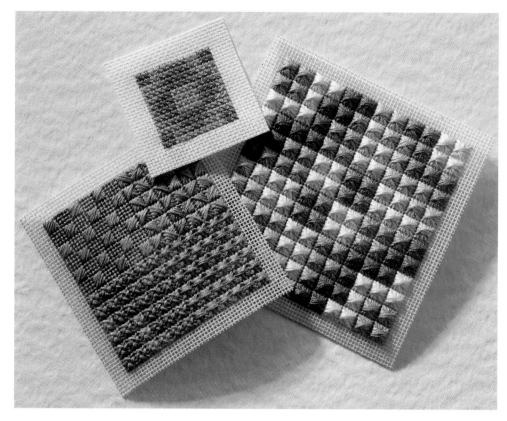

THREE DIFFERENT ways of embroidering a charted geometric design:
TOP – *Cross stitch on evenweave fabric*
LEFT – *Chequer stitch, crossed corners cushion stitch, woven cross stitch and leviathan stitch on single canvas*
RIGHT – *Rhodes stitch on single canvas.*

gently stretch the canvas and secure it with temporary tacks at 2.5 cm (1 in) intervals. Check with a ruler that the canvas is stretched evenly across both width and length, adjust the tacks where necessary, then hammer in all the tacks securely.

4 Moisten the canvas, then leave it out of direct sunlight to dry out thoroughly. This may take anything up a week, depending on the yarn.

COLOUR KNITTING FROM A CROSS STITCH CHART

Small cross stitch designs, especially repeating borders and all-over patterns, can easily be knitted in the same way as Fair Isle knitting, but remember that because each stitch is not perfectly square, your design will appear slightly flattened when it is knitted.

Use the normal Fair Isle techniques of stranding or weaving colours not in use across the back of the knitting. For isolated motifs and designs made up of separate areas of colour, first wind several small balls of each colour. Use a separate ball of yarn to knit each area, twisting the yarns when changing from one colour to another to avoid holes forming.

When knitting from a cross stitch chart, number the chart rows along the right-hand edge, beginning at the bottom. Always read right-side rows (knit rows) from right to left, and wrong side rows (purl rows) from left to right.

FILET CROCHET FROM A CROSS STITCH CHART

Filet crochet is based on a regular grid worked from a chart and it combines basic chain, double crochet and treble stitches. The grid is used as the background for a design which is created by filling in some of the grid spaces with treble stitches.

The crochet fabric can vary from a light, lacy net right through to a close, rather heavy fabric with a solidly-worked pattern. The appearance of the crochet will also depend on your choice of yarn and size of hook. A fine, silky cotton or synthetic thread will create a more delicate effect than, for example, double knitting weight wool. Try out a small sample first to check that you like the effect before embarking on an ambitious project.

ADAPTING THE CHART

Charts for filet crochet show the pattern as it will appear on the right side of the fabric. They are followed from the bottom, working from side to side and reading odd-numbered rows from right to left and even-numbered rows from left to right. Each open square on the chart represents one space on the grid formed by two trebles separated by two chains. Each filled square is worked by replacing the two chains with two trebles to form a solid block of four. Two blocks together on the chart are filled by 7 treble stitches, 3 blocks by 10 stitches, and so on.

You can adapt one of the charts in the book by transferring it square by square onto graph paper. Choose a simple design to begin with, perhaps a letter or flower motif, then decide which areas are to be solid and fill these in with dots on the graph paper. The unmarked squares left indicate the grid background. Number the rows along the right-hand edge, beginning at the lower edge.

WORKING THE CROCHET

Crochet abbreviations: ch = chain, ss = slip stitch, dc = double crochet, tr = treble. (For Amercian readers, dc = single crochet and tr = double crochet.)

1 Begin by making the foundation chain which is not shown on the chart. Simply multiply the number of squares across the chart by 3 and add 1 to find the number of chain stitches you require. Make the foundation chain to this length and begin following the chart from the bottom right-hand corner.

2 When the first square on the chart is a space, add 4 turning chains and work the first tr into the 8th ch from the hook. When the first square is a block, add 2 turning chains and work the first tr into the 4th ch from the hook, then work 1 tr into each of the next 2 ch. Continue along the row from right to left.

DECORATIVE EDGINGS

There are a number of attractive ways to create decorative and unusual edgings for a piece of cross stitch embroidery worked on fabric.

Pin and tack the hem in the usual way, then secure the edge with a row of running stitch (page 22) or back stitch (page 22) in a toning or contrasting colour of embroidery thread. Whipped back stitch (page 22) makes a raised line, which looks almost like thin cord and this can be worked in two colours of thread. For a more ornamental effect, hem by hand (page 152), then stitch either one, two or three rows of spaced alternate cross stitch (page 23) or a narrow border from one of the pattern libraries, working the embroidery just above the hem.

A narrow lace edging may be just the thing to finish off a tablecloth or shelf-edging. You can buy ready-made edging in white, cream and several pastel colours, but it is easy to crochet your own edging. Use one of the fine cotton yarns which are specially spun for crochet and a fine gauge of hook. When you choose a pure cotton yarn, this can be easily dyed at home (page 149) to a matching or contrasting shade. Crochet abbreviations are given above.

LACY PICOT EDGING

Make a chain to the required length, making sure the number of chains is divisible by 3 plus 1.
2 ch, turn.
1st row: 1 tr into 4th ch from hook, 1 tr in each ch to end, turn.
2nd row: ★ 3 ch, miss next 2 tr, 1 dc into next tr, repeat from ★ to end, turn.
3rd row: ss into 1st loop, ★ 6 ch, ss into 4th ch from hook, 2 ch, 1 dc into next loop, repeat from ★ to end. Fasten off.

SAWTOOTH EDGING

Make a chain to the required length, making sure the number of chains is divisible by 4 plus 1.
2 ch, turn.
1st row: 1 tr into 4th ch from hook, 1 tr into each ch to end, turn.
2nd row: 3 ch, 3 tr into edge stitch (first tr), ★ miss 3 tr, 1 dc into next tr, 3 ch, 3 tr into same tr, repeat from ★ to end, ending with miss 3 tr, 1 dc into turning chain. Fasten off.
Carefully starch and press the edgings before slipstitching to the inside of the hem.

DYEING AND PAINTING FABRIC

Fabric paints and dyes can create the perfect background for cross stitch embroidery, especially when stitching a picture.

White or cream fabric is easily dyed at home – use an old, large saucepan or metal bucket and always follow the dye manufacturer's instructions carefully. Take care to rinse surplus dye completely out of the fabric and dry it out of direct sunlight. Cotton and wool fabrics take dyes well, but you will get paler, less vibrant shades on fabric containing a large proportion of synthetic fibres such as polyester or nylon.

When making a background for freestyle embroidery (page 144) experiment by dyeing patterned fabric as

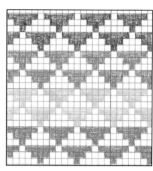

SIMPLE CHARTED designs can be used for other textile techniques as well as cross stitch. Here, the same chart has been worked in filet crochet, cross stitch on evenweave fabric and colour knitting.

well as plain. A large, hectic pattern printed on cotton in many colours can be overdyed with one medium-or dark-toned colour, and this can often produce a subtly shaded and patterned piece of fabric which is perfect to use as the background for a landscape design. You may like to dye cotton and wool threads at the same time as fabric. To do this successfully, before dyeing, wind the yarn round a piece of cardboard to make a skein, then remove the cardboard and tie the skein loosely but securely in several places with separate pieces of thread.

Fabric paints are widely available. Liquid paints can be brushed or sprayed over large areas of fabric. Other paints are applied rather like icing a cake, squeezing the container to force out the contents and make a raised line, while a third type is in crayon form. The paints come in a wide range of colours as well as gold, silver and other metallic shades. First wash, dry and press the fabric to remove any starch or dressing and take care to match fabric and paint successfully. Some paints are suitable only for use with natural fibres like cotton and silk, while other brands can be used on synthetics.

APPLYING FABRIC PAINTS

1 Work on a flat surface protected by layers of newspaper and stick the edges of the fabric down with masking tape to prevent it moving and smearing the paint. Alternatively, pin or staple your fabric to a wooden stretcher (page 20).

2 Use liquid paints straight from the container after shaking or stirring thoroughly, or mix several colours together to create your own shades.

3 Work in sections across the fabric, allowing each colour to dry completely before applying the next one. Wash out your brushes thoroughly when changing from one colour to another.

4 Fabric paints can be intermixed to give a wide range of colours. Mixing opaque white with bright colours will give you a range of pastels with good covering power, but avoid diluting paints with large amounts of water so that they become runny and difficult to handle.

5 Paints which are applied by squeezing the container are used to draw lines and dashes, squiggles and blobs. Practise first on a scrap of paper, squeezing the container gently as you draw it slowly across the surface.

6 Fabric crayons give a more subtle effect than the other types of paints. Individual colours can be shaded and blended easily into each other.

7 Whatever type of fabric paint you choose, fix the colours before starting to stitch by following the individual manufacturer's instructions.

CHAPTER NINE

TECHNICAL SKILLS

SEWING STITCHES

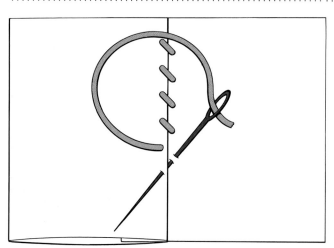

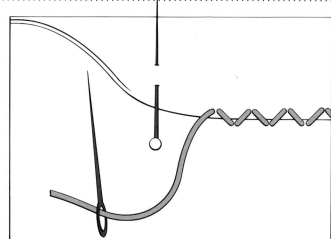

HEMMING STITCH Secure the thread inside the fold of the hem with a few tiny stitches. Take small slanting stitches through both the fabric and hem in one movement, as shown. Pick up one or two fabric threads with each stitch and space the stitches evenly along the hem.

SLIPSTITCH Use slipstitch to secure the edge of bias binding or to join two folds of fabric together.

Secure the thread inside the fold and bring the needle out. Slip the needle along inside the fold then pick up a few threads of the fabric. Gently pull the thread to close the stitches and repeat along the row. When using slipstitch to join two pieces of fabric, work the stitch alternately from one fold to the other in the same way.

MAKING A HEM

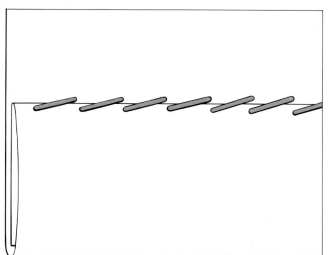

DOUBLE HEM Make a narrow double hem when working with fine fabrics, around small items such as napkins, and also where you need a firm edge. Fold over half the total hem allowance and press in position, then fold over the same amount again and press. Make sure the corners are folded over neatly, then pin and tack in position and secure with hemming stitch (above) or a row of machine stitching.

UNEVEN WIDTH HEM Use this hem on medium and heavyweight fabrics. Fold over the total amount allowed for the hem and press in position. Turn under 6 mm (¼ in) of the raw edge and press. Pin and tack hem in position and secure with hemming stitch (*above*) or machine stitching.

FINISHING CORNERS

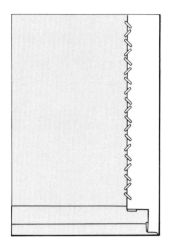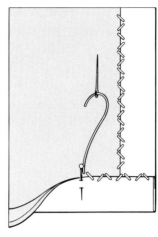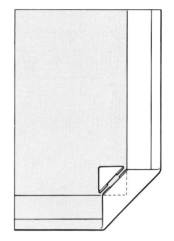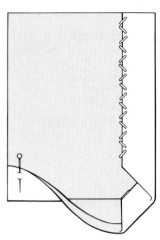

STRAIGHT CORNER Trim away the excess fabric at the corner of an uneven hem to reduce bulk.

1 Fold over and press the hem, and hem one side by hand (page 152), beginning about 5 cm (2 in) from the first corner. Unfold the corner and cut away a rectangle of fabric, as shown.

2 Fold the hem back into position and continue hemming. Repeat at each corner.

MITRED CORNER Mitre the corners of a wide hem to reduce bulk and give a neat finish.

1 Fold the hem and press in position. Unfold the hem once, then press the corner over as shown so that the diagonal fold falls exactly across the corner of the hemline crease. Cut off the corner.

2 Fold over one side along the hemline crease, press and pin in position. Fold over the other side. Stitch the hem, then slipstitch (page 152) the edges of the mitre together.

MAKING BIAS BINDING

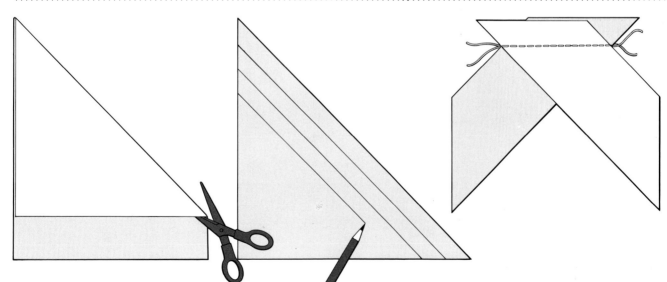

Ready-made bias binding is available or you can cut your own from matching or contrasting fabric.

1 Find the bias of the fabric by laying it flat and folding over one corner at an angle of 45° to the selvedge. Cut along the fold.

2 Decide on the finished width of the binding, adding 6 mm (¼ in) to each edge for turnings, and mark parallel lines on the fabric to this width. Working from the cut edge, mark the

lines on the fabric with a ruler and dressmaker's pencil. Cut out the strips.

3 Join the strips together by placing two strips at right angles with right sides facing, as shown. Pin and stitch them together, taking a 6 mm (¼ in) seam allowance. Press the seam open and trim off the surplus triangular shapes. Fold 6 mm (¼ in) to the wrong side down each long edge and press.

APPLYING BIAS BINDING

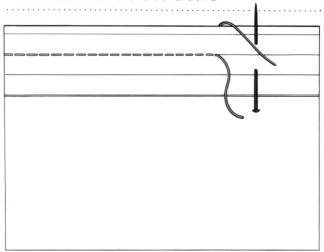
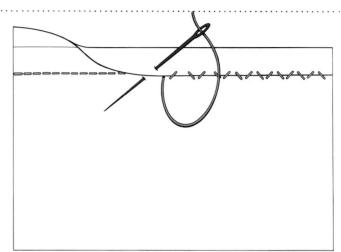

1 With the right side of the fabric facing, open out the binding and place the raw edge level with the raw edge of the fabric. Machine stitch along the fold line.

2 Fold binding over onto the wrong side of the fabric, enclosing the raw edge. Pin in place and slipstitch (page 152) along the stitched line.

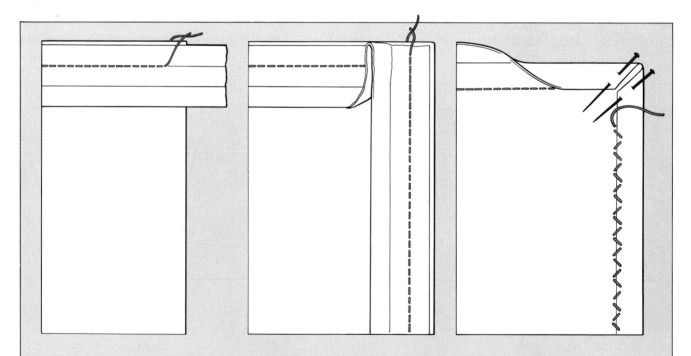

BINDING A CORNER

1 Pin the binding along the first side and machine stitch in place, beginning about 5 cm (2 in) from the first corner. End the stitching the same distance in from the corner as the row of stitching is from the edge of the fabric. Work a few stitches to secure the thread and cut off the ends.

2 Fold the unstitched binding back on itself and then down the adjacent side to form a flap. Make sure the top fold lies squarely along the raw edge of the fabric. Continue stitching along this edge, taking care that the flap does not get caught in the stitching. Repeat these two steps at each corner.

3 Turn over the binding on to the wrong side. This will form a mitre on the right side. Pin the corners in place on the wrong side, taking a tuck in the binding as shown. Slipstitch (page 152) along the folded edge.

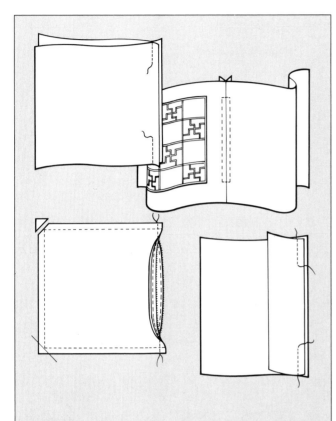

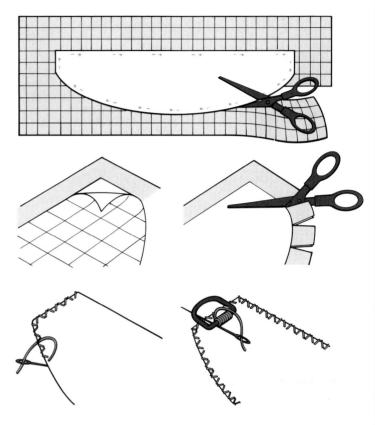

MAKING A PLAIN CUSHION COVER

The simplest way to make a plain cushion cover is to stitch the front and back pieces together round the edge, leaving an opening along one side. Slipstitch (page 152) the opening closed after the filling has been added. Use this method to make the pot-pourri sachets, page 88, and the pincushions, page 122. On a larger cushion, it looks neater to close the opening with a zip fastener.

1 Pin the front and back together and stitch about 5 cm (2 in) at either end of the opening. Press the seams flat.

2 Pin, tack and machine stitch the zip fastener along the opening.

3 Open the zip fastener and stitch round the remaining three sides of the cushion. Clip the corners to reduce bulk, then turn to the right side and press.

4 When the cushion front has been embroidered right to the edge, insert the zip fastener in a seam across the cushion back for a really neat finish. Make a frilled or piped cover in the same way. Position the seam either centrally or at one side of the fabric, stitching about 5 cm (2 in) at each end.

5 Follow step 2, above. Then open the zip fastener, place front and back together with right sides facing and stitch round all four sides. Clip the corners, then turn to the right side and press.

MAKING A PAIR OF TIE-BACKS

1 Make a paper pattern by selecting one of the templates on page 157, tracing it and enlarging it to the correct size. Pin the paper pattern onto doubled-sided, self-adhesive pelmet stiffener and cut around the shape twice. Also cut two shapes from the lining fabric, but this time add 1 cm (½ in) all round for turnings.

2 Peel the plain backing away from one side of the stiffener and position it on the wrong side of the embroidered fabric, leaving an even margin of fabric all the way round. Then turn the fabric over and smooth over with your fingers to eliminate any creases. Peel the graphed backing away from the stiffener.

3 Cut notches round the curved edge of the fabric, as shown, and fold the fabric over onto the self-adhesive surface of the stiffener, smoothing out any creases. Fold over the long straight edge and then the short edges.

4 Position the lining over the same side of the tie-back and stick in place. Turn under the raw edges of the lining all the way round, notching the curved edge, and slipstitch (page 152) to the embroidered fabric. Repeat steps 2, 3 and 4 to make the second tie-back.

5 Sew a brass D ring onto the lining at each end of the tie-backs. Fix a tie-back hook securely in position at each side of the window, then hang up the tie-backs.

MAKING A CAFÉ CURTAIN

MAKING A PAPER PATTERN Decide on the size of the scallops at the top of the curtain and cut a template from thin card. Cut a piece of dressmaker's paper 20 cm (8 in) deep and the same width as the finished curtain. Beginning at the centre of the paper, mark evenly spaced scallop shapes along the top, leaving about 5 cm (2 in) between each scallop and the same amount at each end of the paper. Cut out the paper pattern.

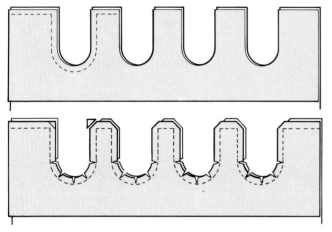

MAKING THE CURTAIN

1 Pin the paper pattern to the top of the curtain and cut out the scallops. Repeat along the top of the facing. Turn a narrow hem along the long straight edge of the facing and machine stitch. With right sides together and raw edges matching, pin the scalloped facing to the scalloped edge of the curtain. Tack along the scallops, then machine stitch 6 mm (¼ in) from the raw edge.

2 Notch each curve and clip the corners to reduce bulk. Turn to the right side and press carefully. Turn under the raw side edges of the facing and slipstitch (page 152) to the hemmed edges of the curtain. If you are not using brass clips to hang the curtains, stitch a café curtain ring to the centre of the spaces between each pair of scallops and one at each end of the curtain.

FRAMING PICTURES

LACING OVER CARD Before framing, mount your picture over a piece of thick cardboard. Use a strong thread which will not snap easily, such as buttonhole thread, linen carpet thread or very fine string.

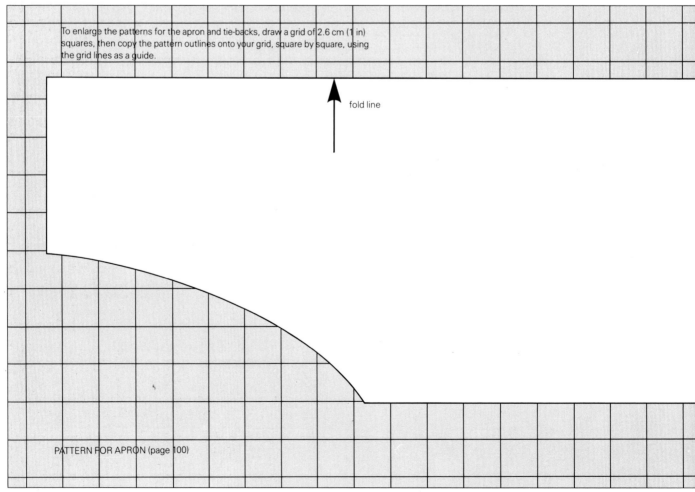

To enlarge the patterns for the apron and tie-backs, draw a grid of 2.6 cm (1 in) squares, then copy the pattern outlines onto your grid, square by square, using the grid lines as a guide.

fold line

PATTERN FOR APRON (page 100)

1 Cut the cardboard to the required size, allowing a little extra all round so that any embroidered areas at the edge of the picture will not be hidden by the rebate (overlapping lip) of the frame. Place the fabric right side up over the card, fold over the top and secure with pins pushed right into the edge of the cardboard. Repeat along the bottom, taking care to keep the fabric grain straight.

2 Using a long piece of thread, take long stitches between the two fabric edges, starting at the top left. When you have reached the bottom, remove the pins. Knot the thread at the starting point, then move downwards from stitch to stitch, tightening them as you go. Secure the thread end.

3 Repeat the pinning and lacing along the remaining two sides, folding in the corners and tightening the stitches.

FRAMING There are several options: a wooden stretcher, simple clip or conventional picture frame, with or without glass. Each has its disadvantages – the stretcher will not protect the embroidery from dust and dirt, while a glazed frame tends to obscure the texture of the stitching. The glass of clip frames flattens the stitches.

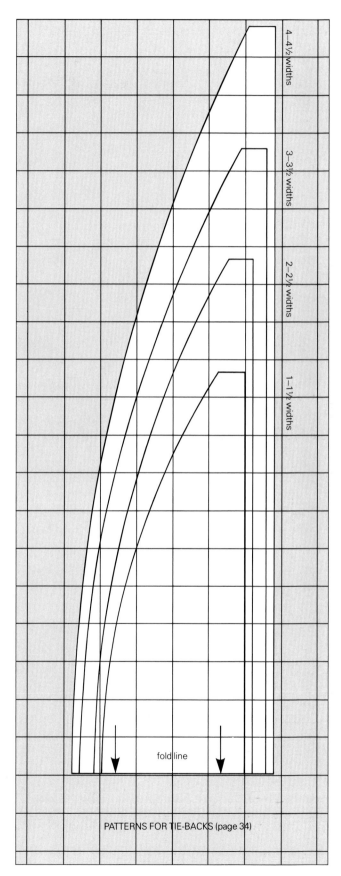

PATTERNS FOR TIE-BACKS (page 34)

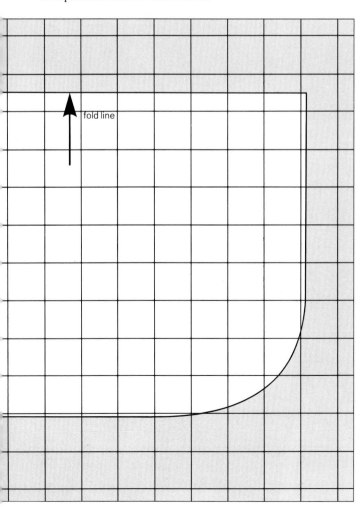

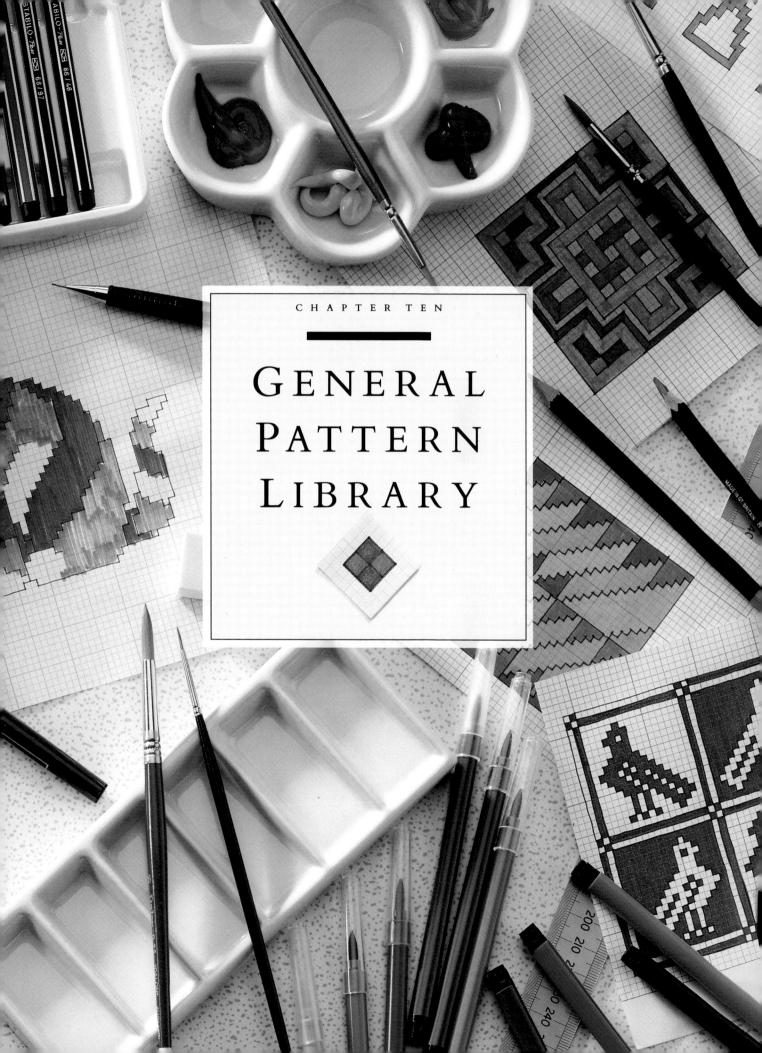

CHAPTER TEN

GENERAL PATTERN LIBRARY

Alphabets and Numbers

Alphabets and Numbers

abcdefghijklmno pqrstuvwxyz

ABCDEFGHIJKLMN
OPQRSTUVWXYZ **

ABCDEFGHIJKLMN
OPQRSTUVWXYZ

1234567890

ABCDEFGHIJKL
MNOPQRSTUV
WXYZ

123456789

Alphabets and Numbers

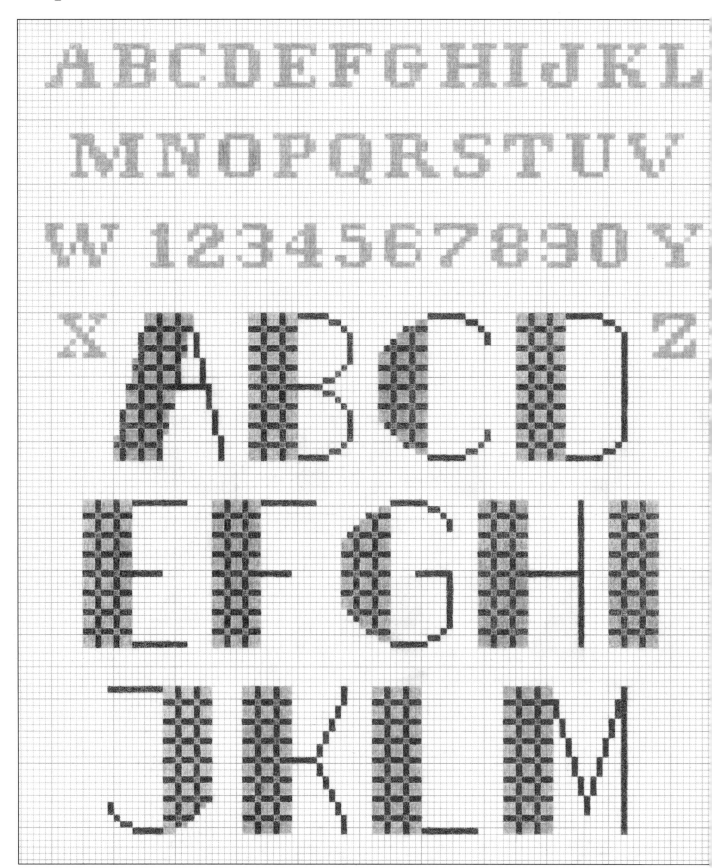

Alphabets

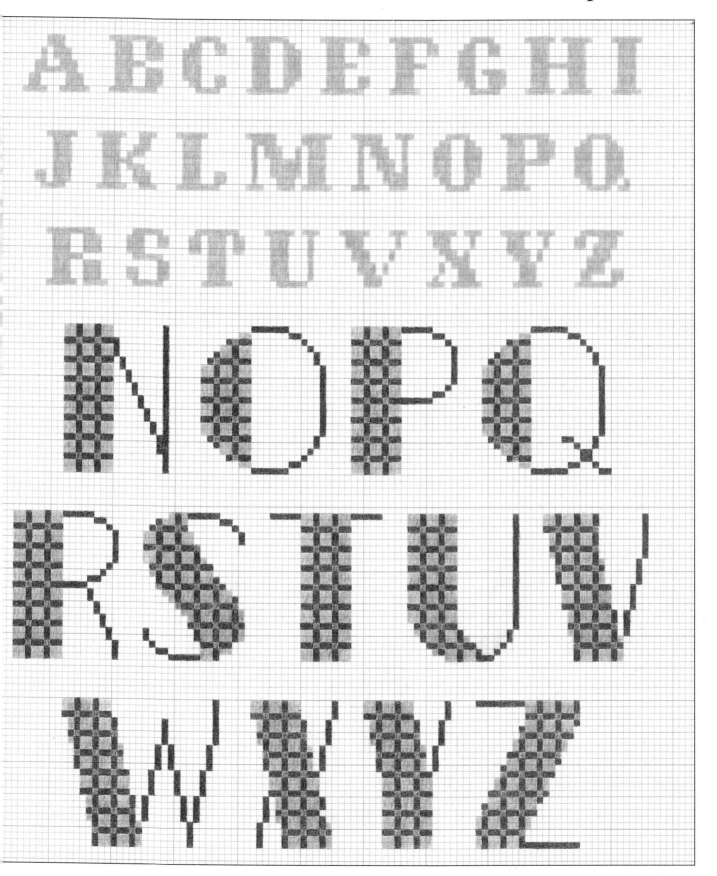

Zodiac Symbols, Hearts and Bows

Aries · Taurus · Gemini · Cancer · Leo

Virgo · Libra · Scorpio · Sagittarius · Capricorn

Aquarius · Pisces

Greetings Cards and Tree Decorations

Tree Borders and All-over Patterns

Decorative Edgings and Frames

Fruit and Foliage Borders

Geometric Borders and All-over Patterns

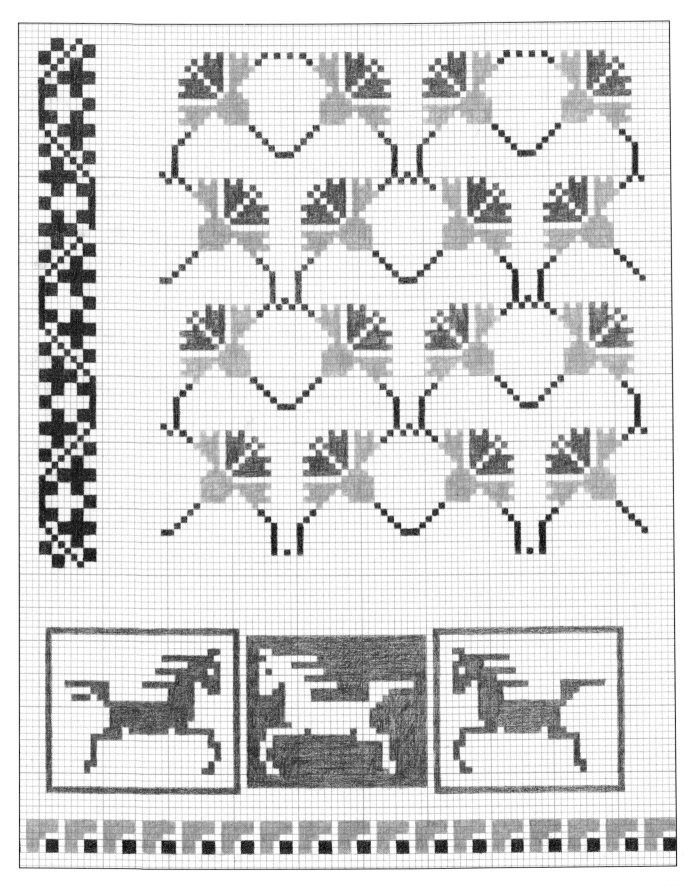

Geometric Borders

Geometric Borders

Geometric Repeat Patterns

Geometric Repeat Patterns

Glossary

AIDA An *evenweave* fabric woven so that an identical number of vertical and horizontal woven blocks are produced over a given area.

AINRING Similar to *Aida*, but with a larger number of woven blocks to every 2.5 cm (1 in).

APPLIED WORK *see appliqué.*

APPLIQUÉ A textile technique in which one fabric is placed on top of another and secured with tiny stitches.

ART DECO A style of decoration fashionable during the 1920s and 1930s and characterized by geometric shapes, symmetrical designs and bold colours.

ART NOUVEAU A style of design during the 1890s characterized by flowing, sinuous lines and stylized natural forms.

BERLIN WOOLWORK A type of embroidery worked in cross stitch from a printed *chart* with brightly coloured wools. Originating in Germany, woolwork became very popular throughout Europe and the United States during the 1800s.

BLACKWORK A favourite embroidery technique of the sixteenth century which is still in use today. Outline and filling stitches are worked in black or a dark-coloured thread on *evenweave* linen to create geometric and stylized designs.

BLOCKING A finishing process for *needlepoint* where the embroidered *canvas* is moistened with water, pinned out to shape and left to dry.

BORDER A band of embroidery always used on the straight.

CANVAS A woven material constructed from stiffened threads and used as the basis for *needlepoint*. The *warp* and *weft* threads make a regular grid.

CANVASWORK *see needlepoint.*

CHART An embroidery design expressed as coloured squares on *graph paper* and worked by counting threads. Sometimes symbols are used instead of coloured squares to denote different thread colours.

COLOUR KNITTING Knitting decorated with a pattern worked in two or more colours of yarn in each row.

COTTON PERLE *see pearl cotton.*

COUNT The number of threads or woven blocks which can be stitched in 2.5 cm (1 in) of *evenweave* fabric. Also applied to *canvas* and known as the gauge.

COUNTED THREAD EMBROIDERY A term applied to any embroidery technique on fabric which is worked by counting the *warp* and *weft* threads to determine the size and position of each stitch.

CREWEL WOOL A tightly twisted, fine wool thread for both embroidery and *needlepoint*, always used as a single thread.

CUT AND DRAWN WORK *see cutwork* and *drawn thread work.*

CUTWORK A group of embroidery techniques in which patterns are outlined with buttonhole stitch and then the fabric is cut away in various parts of the design. Often grouped with *drawn thread work* and known as cut and drawn work.

DARNING STITCH A simple in-and-out stitch used to repair a hole in fabric, or worked evenly to produce an ornamental design.

DOUBLE CANVAS *Canvas* in which the regular grid is formed by pairs of vertical and horizontal threads. Also known as Penelope canvas.

DRAWN THREAD WORK A group of embroidery techniques in which threads are withdrawn from the fabric and the spaces left are then filled or edged with embroidery stitches, eg *Hardanger embroidery*. Often grouped with *cutwork* and known collectively as cut and drawn work.

EMBROIDERY FLOSS *see stranded cotton.*

EVENWEAVE FABRIC Fabric with *warp* and *weft* threads of identical thickness which provide the same number of vertical and horizontal threads or woven blocks over a given area.

FILET CROCHET A type of crochet in which the solidly worked design contrasts with a net background.

FRAME An adjustable rectangular frame for stretching fabric and *canvas* while embroidery stitches are being worked.

FREESTYLE EMBROIDERY Any embroidery worked freely on fabric in which the *warp* and *weft* threads are not counted to act as a guide for the stitching.

GAUGE *see count.*

GRAPH PAPER Paper with a printed grid of equidistant vertical and horizontal lines.

HARDANGER EMBROIDERY A *drawn thread work* technique originally from Norway which is worked on coarse *evenweave* linen with thick threads.

HOOP A two-part round frame for stretching fabric while embroidery stitches are being worked.

INTERLOCK CANVAS *Canvas* in which the threads are interlocked to form a very stable grid.

METAL THREAD EMBROIDERY Various embroidery techniques using silver, gold and other metallic threads.

MONO CANVAS *see single canvas.*

MOTIF Part of a design which can be isolated as a single unit. A motif can be used alone, or repeated to build up *borders* and all-over patterns.

NEEDLEPOINT A term denoting embroidery on *canvas*. Usually, all the canvas threads are completely covered by the embroidery stitches. Needlepoint is also known as canvaswork.

PATTERN DARNING A type of embroidery in which the design is worked in evenly spaced *darning-stitches.*

PEARL COTTON A tightly twisted embroidery thread with a lustre which cannot be divided into separate strands.

PENELOPE CANVAS *see double canvas.*

PERSIAN WOOL A thick, loosely twisted wool thread for *needlepoint* which can be divided into three separate strands.

SAMPLER Originally a piece of embroidery worked to experiment with new stitches, patterns and techniques. Later, the sampler became an educational exercise for generations of schoolgirls to practise spelling and embroidery skills.

SINGLE CANVAS *Canvas* in which the regular grid is formed by single vertical and horizontal threads. Also known as mono canvas.

SOFT EMBROIDERY COTTON A thick, twisted embroidery thread with a matt finish which cannot be separated into separate strands.

STRANDED COTTON A loosely twisted embroidery thread with a slight sheen which consists of six separate strands. The thread can be divided and individual strands combined into various thicknesses.

STRETCHER A rectangular wooden frame which cannot be adjusted, used for embroidery and *needlepoint*.

TAPESTRY A term which describes a type of hand weaving. The name is often wrongly applied to *needlepoint*.

TAPESTRY NEEDLE A blunt-ended needle used for working *needlepoint* and *counted thread embroidery*.

TAPESTRY WOOL A thick, tightly twisted pure wool yarn mainly used for *needlepoint*.

WARP Threads running lengthways down a piece of woven fabric at right angles to the *weft*.

WASTE CANVAS *Canvas* tacked onto fabric to provide a grid for working cross stitch accurately. Special waste canvas is available, or substitute either *single* or *double canvas*, but not *interlock canvas*.

WEFT Threads running widthways across a piece of woven fabric at right angles to the *warp*.

Index